SideKick
Version 1.0

BORLAND INTERNATIONAL Inc.
4585 Scotts Valley Drive
Scotts Valley, CA 95066
U.S.A.

CONTENTS

INTRODUCTION

FAST TRACK

SIDEKICK APPLICATION

SIDEKICK ACCESSORIES

PRINTMANAGER

APPENDIX A

APPENDIX B

INDEX

INTRODUCTION

SideKick™ is a collection of desktop organization programs that operate concurrently with other Macintosh™ software. The programs that make up SideKick are often referred to as *accessories*. They reside in the Apple® pull-down menu, and are accessible with almost all Macintosh programs.

SideKick is *more* than a group of accessories. It also has several applications. When used as a start-up disk, all of the accessories are available from the Apple pull-down menu, while the SideKick main display presents an expanded version of the personal information, telephone and time management programs.

SideKick also features an extremely powerful printing application. PrintManager is designed to sort and print SideKick's PhoneBook files in a variety of different formats, including index cards, mailing labels, and phonebooks of various sizes and formats. (Week-at-a-Peek and QuikSheets can be printed using Borland's Traveling SideKick™ for the Macintosh.) All of the clutter that once occupied your desktop can be compiled and printed from SideKick's desktop.

SideKick includes two other utilities that you'll undoubtedly find useful. One utility is used to convert MacPhone™, Habadex™ and similar type data base files (i.e., ASCII text files) into SideKick PhoneBook files. The other utility, the QuikSheets Editor, is used to create up to 21 custom sheets for the QuikSheets accessory.

The programs that make up SideKick are fully integrated. Since related accessories and applications share common data files, information is automatically distributed to many of the programs. In addition, SideKick utilizes the Macintosh clipboard for copying and pasting between accessories, as well as *to* and *from* other applications.

With SideKick, you will become more organized. Essential information about the people you know or do business with will be stored in the PhoneBook files. Phone numbers from these files can be automatically dialed through PhoneLink™, the interface cable used to connect your Macintosh to any standard telephone. Telephone activities, including person, duration, cost, consulting fees and phone notes are automatically recorded in the PhoneLog. Appointments can be scheduled into Week-at-a-Peek, the CalendarBook, Things-To-Do and multiple Alarms. All of this is performed while operating ''behind'' other Macintosh applications.

SideKick's other ''background'' features include:

Notepad+—a mini word processor that produces MacWrite™ and Word™ compatible documents. Edit commands and search features are fully supported.

ReadiPrinter—a software spooling program that frees up your mouse and keyboard while printing any Macintosh text file.

Calculator+—a multi-function business calculator featuring a paper-tape to screen and printer.

MacTerm—Hayes-compatible terminal software for 300, 1200 or 2400 baud modems. Fully integrated with Notepad+ for sending, retrieving and editing data.

Area Code Lookup—time zone and locality information for all area codes.

MacClock—analog clock featuring a sweep-second hand.

Credit Cards—a record of credit card information including balances and limits.

Expenses—a record of business and travel expenses.

About This Manual

This manual will provide you with a complete understanding of SideKick—first as an application, then as an accessory. This will be followed by instructions for using the desktop utilities, such as PrintManager and Copy PhoneBook.

What will *not* be discussed are the various concepts, mouse skills and terminology that have become a part of the Macintosh world. If you are unfamiliar with the following terms, review your Macintosh owner's guide or the Macintosh guided tour:

- ☐ **Icons**
- ☐ **Mouse**
- ☐ **Point, Click, Drag, Double-Click**
- ☐ **Windows**
- ☐ **Elevators**
- ☐ **Scroll Bars**
- ☐ **Pull-down menus**
- ☐ **Opening and saving documents**
- ☐ **Control Panel**
- ☐ **System clock**
- ☐ **Finder**

The chapter *Fast Track*, is designed for those who are very familiar with these terms and with Macintosh software. It consists of short descriptions with labeled screen displays which provide a quick way to learn SideKick. **Help** screens are available to supplement the Fast Track descriptions. For Sidekick's application program, **Help** screens are presented by choosing ***About SideKick...*** from the **Apple** pull-down menu; **Help** screens for the accessories are presented by choosing the ***About...*** command in each accessory menu. More detailed explanations of SideKick's applications and accessories are provided in subsequent chapters.

Before Beginning

Before we begin, take a moment to fill out the attached warranty card which is provided for your protection. This card is the only way of ensuring you a replacement disk should anything happen to your master. The card also ensures that you receive information about program updates and new products from Borland.

Backup Disk

For your protection, you should make a backup copy of the SideKick distribution disk. Include your data files on this disk if they will fit, or you can use a separate disk for your data files. All of your data files should be contained on the same disk so you can easily track them.

Hard Disk

SideKick is designed to operate on most popular hard disk systems. Follow the instructions provided in Appendix A for mounting SideKick on your hard disk.

Start-Up

To begin using SideKick:

■ **Turn the Macintosh power switch to ON and insert the SideKick master disk into the internal disk drive.**

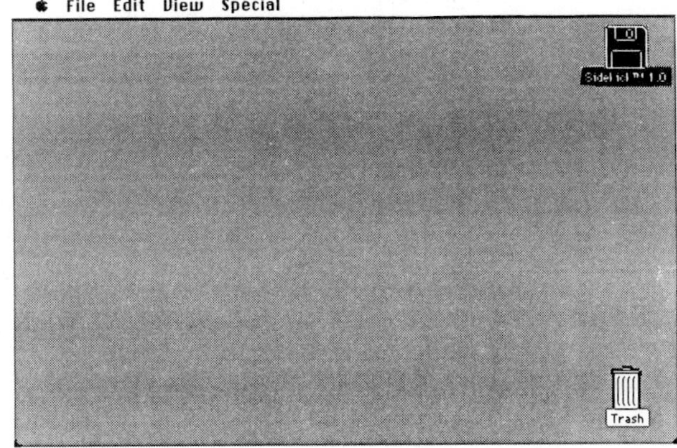

The SideKick disk icon will appear in the top right corner of your screen.

■ **Double-click the SideKick disk icon to reveal the desktop.**

Creating A Data Disk

SideKick data files can be maintained either on the same disk with the SideKick utilities, or on a separate data disk if there is not enough room. Wherever your data files exist, they must reside on the same disk as the DataPhiles folder.

Since SideKick creates and maintains real-time information files (i.e., CalendarBook appointments, PhoneLog, etc.), it is essential that you keep such information in one place—on a data disk. Maintaining a single data disk will prevent you from misplacing or scattering your SideKick data. Of course it's essential to always back-up your data disk.

With SideKick's desktop displayed:

- **Insert a blank disk into the external disk drive.**
- **Initialize and name the disk.**
- **Point to the folder on SideKick's desktop titled DataPhiles, click, hold and drag to the data disk icon. Release.**

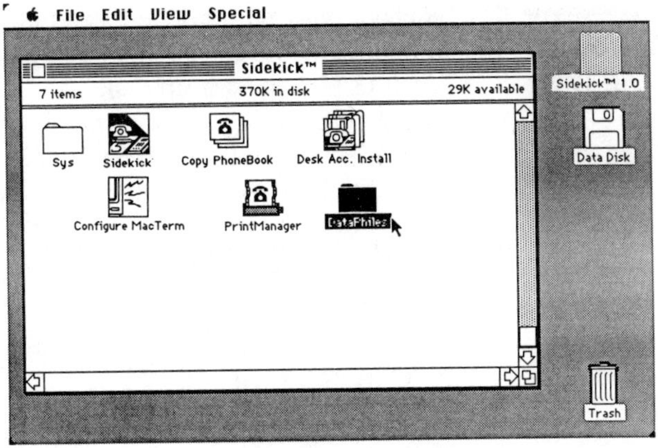

The folder and its contents will be copied to the data disk. The DataPhiles folder contains all of SideKick's data files. Since this folder is essential for operating SideKick, repeat the above procedure to create a back-up data disk. Store one of these data disks away for safekeeping, and use it only as a master copy for creating future data disks.

After (and only after) creating the data disks, *trash* the DataPhiles folder from the SideKick master disk:

- **Point to the DataPhiles folder on the SideKick desktop, click, hold and drag to the trash can. Release.**
- **Choose *Empty Trash* from the Special pull-down menu.**

SideKick Desktop

SideKick may be used as a stand-alone program, containing the necessary elements of any start-up disk. When used as a start-up disk, the SideKick master disk should be placed in the internal disk drive and the data disk in the external drive. The standard procedure for using SideKick as a start-up disk is:

1. **Turn the Macintosh power switch to ON and insert the SideKick master disk into the internal disk drive.**

The SideKick disk icon will appear at the top right corner of your screen.

2. **Insert the data disk containing the DataPhiles folder into the external disk drive.**

The data disk will appear below the master disk icon.

3. **Double-click the SideKick master disk icon to reveal its desktop.**

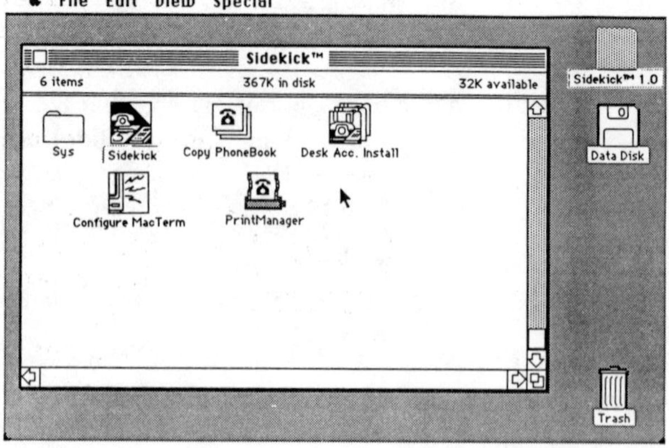

All of SideKick's applications and utilities are available on the master disk desktop. The files they access are stored on the data disk, inside the DataPhiles folder. As with most Macintosh programs, specific applications are accessed by double-clicking the appropriate desktop icon. Specific data files to be used by an application (i.e., a specific PhoneBook file) are selected by double-clicking that particular data file icon on the data disk desktop.

The applications and utilities present on the SideKick master disk include:

SideKick–Application used for full operation of SideKick's personal information, time management and telecommunications pro-programs. Also serves as the primary source for data input into the PhoneBook files and for creating new PhoneBooks.

Copy PhoneBook–Application for copying selected PhoneBook entries when creating new PhoneBooks. An option is provided to produce an abbreviated version of the original, which includes only *name, number* and *category.*

Desk Accessory Installer-A utility used to install any number of SideKick's accessories onto other Macintosh applications. The installed accessories reside in the Apple pull-down menu of the target application disk.

Configure MacTerm- A utility used to configure MacTerm for your specific modem and communication needs.

PrintManager—A comprehensive printing application designed to sort and print the PhoneBook files in a variety of formats, including index cards, mailing labels, and mail merge with MicroSoft's Word™.

With the desktop displayed, you may choose one of two ways to learn SideKick. You can proceed with the following chapter, called *Fast Track*, which is a concise, pictorial description of SideKick, *or* for a more detailed explanation, you can skip this section and go directly to SideKick Application.

FAST TRACK

This section is designed for those who are familiar with the Macintosh and its software and want to get up and running immediately. Presented are the screen displays and abbreviated descriptions of the applications and accessories that make up SideKick.

To begin this chapter, be sure that the SideKick master disk is placed in the internal disk drive and your Data disk in the external drive.

■ **Double-click the SideKick icon to open the application.**

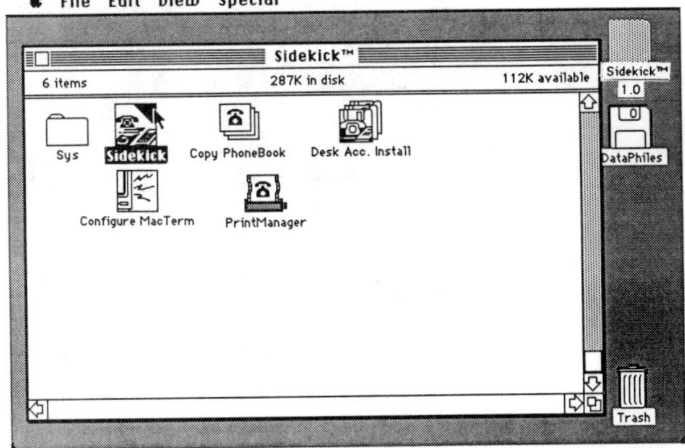

*Note: A series of **Help** screens for operating the SideKick application are available by choosing **About SideKick** from the **Apple** pull-down menu.*

SideKick Main Display

This is SideKick's application main display. Note the following parts:

Long Distance box is used to select or deselect the use of the long distance service checked-off in the **Services** pull-down menu.

Incoming box is used to designate a call as incoming. If checked, the call will be logged as [in] and phone charges will not be calculated.

Active name window—tells you who you're calling.

Time-stamp and billing displayed here.

PhoneBook filename listed here. PhoneBooks can be changed from the **Goodies** pull-down menu.

Active number window—tells you the number that is being dialed.

Dialing status window—tells you when to pick-up the phone, etc.

Manual dialing pad—clicking these buttons will generate dial tones.

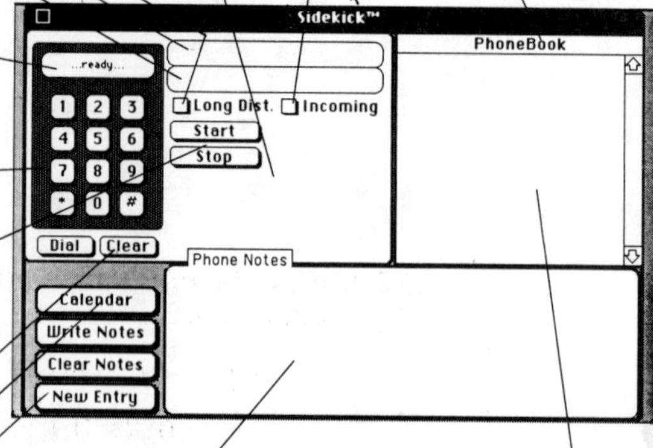

Start and **Stop** button are used to accurately time the call. Clicking the Stop button will rcord the call to the PhoneLog.

Clear is used to clear the active name and number windows.

Calendar is used to bring up the monthly Calendarbook or Week-at-a-Peek.

New Entry is used to enter new names into the current PhoneBook.

Phone Notes is always available for jotting down notes about a call. Clicking the **Write Notes** button will append the notes to the PhoneLog. **Clear Notes** will clear the Phone Notes window.

PhoneBook window will display all entries in the selected PhoneBook. It can be viewed alphabetically by *name* or by *category* as selected from the **Goodies** pull-down menu. Names may be selected for dialing here: Click the name and then the **Dial** button. Information about the person you're calling is temporarily displayed in the PhoneBook window.

Edit pull-down menu is used to Cut, Copy and Paste information to other Macintosh applications and accessories.

Services pull-down menu is used for entering long distance services.

PhoneBook pull-down menu is used for entering long distance services.

Goodies pull-down menu is used for a variety of telephone operations.
The important items include:
Log Calls—if checked will record all calls to the PhoneLog after clicking the **Stop** button for each call.
Sort by Name or by Category—displays the PhoneBook alphabetically by name or category.
Change Area Code—designates your particular area code.
Examine PhoneLog—brings up the PhoneLog window.
Change PhoneBooks—presents a file menu of your PhoneBooks for you to choose for display.

- **Choose *Change Area Code* from the Goodies pull-down menu.**

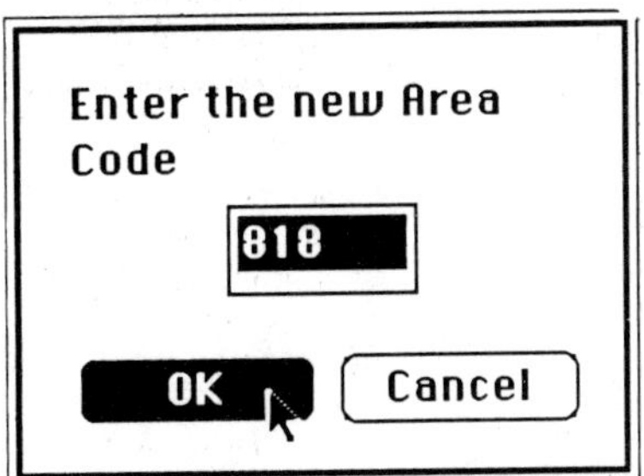

- **Enter your specific area code and click the close box.**
- **Click the New Entry button.**

PhoneBook Entry Card

Each PhoneBook entry requires you to fill out a personal index card with the following information:

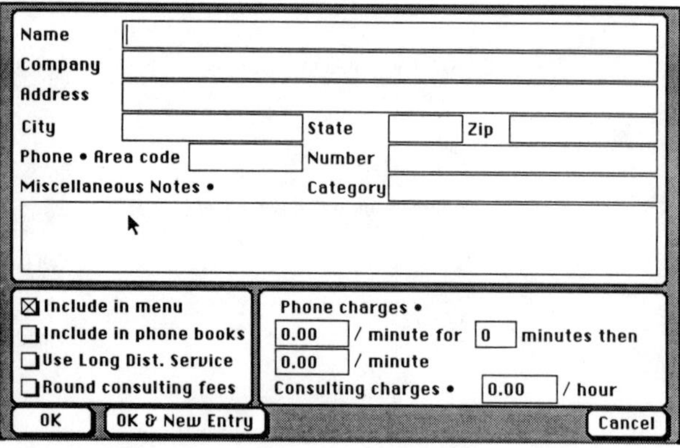

Filling out an index card is quite easy. Simply type in the *name* (last name first) and press Tab to enter the *company* field. Repeat for each field. To determine phone charges, consult your telephone book or call your local operator. Click the *include in menu* option if it is a number that you'll be calling often. When completed:

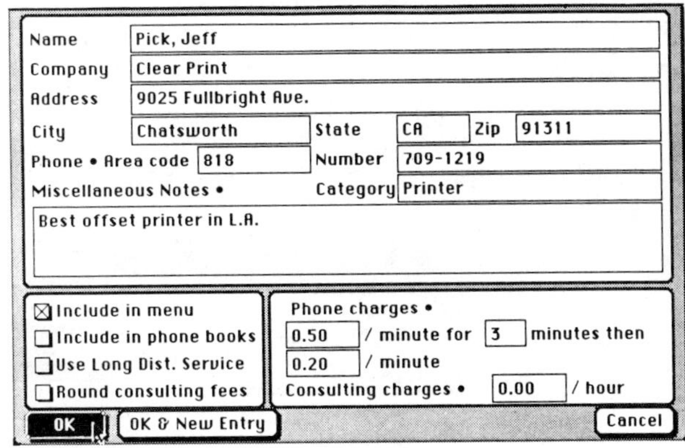

■ **Click the OK button.**

You will return to the main display with the new entry listed in the PhoneBook window and pull-down menu.

Additional names can be entered in the same manner. If you want to make numerous entries, click the **OK & New Entry** button at the bottom of the index card to display another blank card.

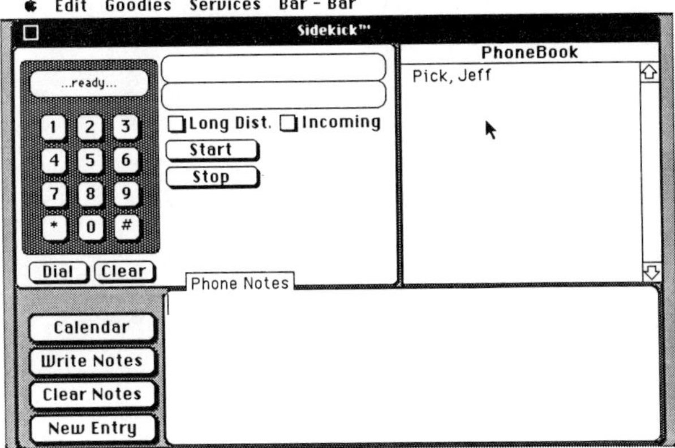

Dialing Phone Numbers

PhoneBook entries can be dialed in one of two ways: The quickest method is to simply *choose* a name from the PhoneBook pull-down menu. The selected name will appear in the active name window, the phone number in the active number window and instructions to "Pick up phone" in the status window.

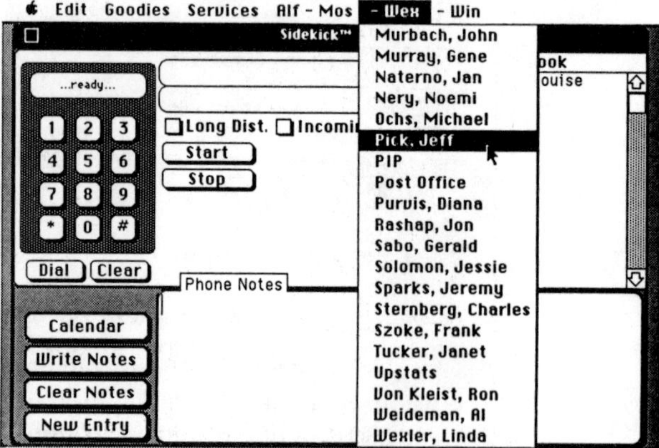

The other method is two-step: Click a name in the PhoneBook window and click the **Dial** button. This method has the advantage of temporarily displaying the personal information about the person you're dialing.

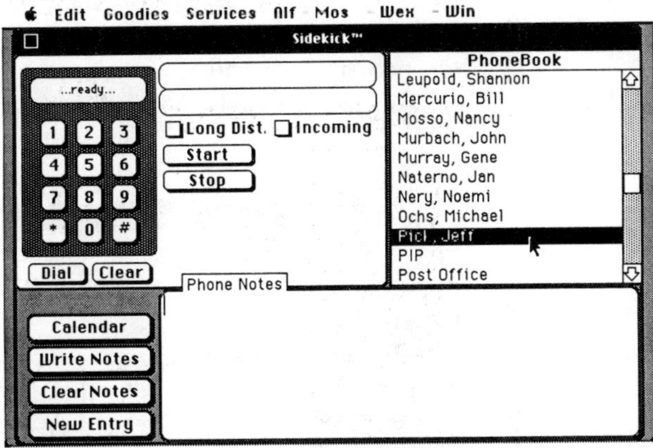

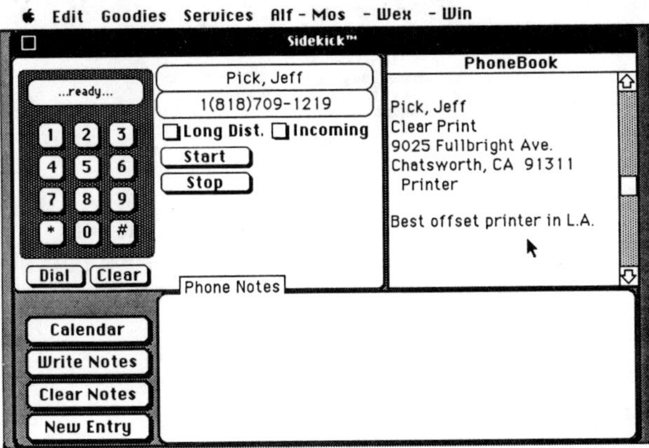

Numbers can also be dialed manually by clicking the numbered keypad, or by typing the number into the active number field and clicking **Dial**.

Recording The Call

The information about the phone call can be recorded in SideKick's PhoneLog. When the call is answered, click the **Start** button to set the starting time. Type any notes about your conversation in the Phone Notes window. After completing your note, click the **Write Notes** button to copy the notes to the PhoneLog. At the end of each call, hang up and click the **Stop** button to stop the time and billing recorder and copy all of the information to the PhoneLog.

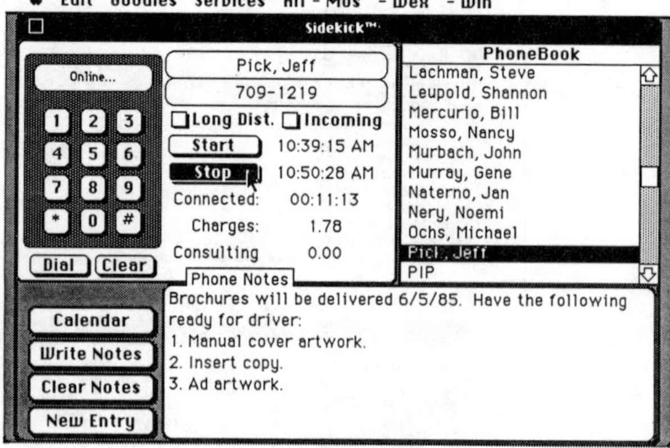

To view and print your PhoneLog choose *Examine PhoneLog* from the **Goodies** pull-down menu.

Sort By Category

Your PhoneBook can be sorted and displayed by *category*. This option is available in the **Goodies** pull-down menu.

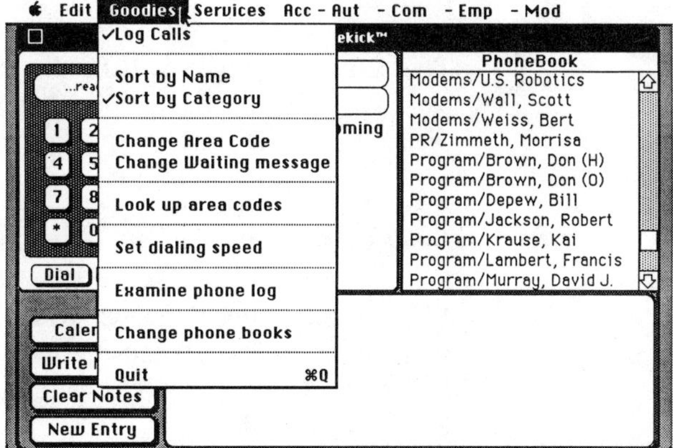

PhoneBooks sorted by category are displayed with the category preceding the name.

CalendarBook

Calendar events and activities can be entered into SideKick's CalendarBook and Week-at-a-Peek by clicking the **Calendar** button (or by choosing *CalendarBook* from the **Apple** pull-down menu).

The screen displayed will be the one which was last closed. Each calendar display has a custom pull-down menu where the other display can be selected.

The Monthly Calendar displays the entire month for any year from 1905 to 2030. Any day of the month can be clicked to present its daily notepage at the bottom of the display. It is here where events are entered by typing from the keyboard or pasting from another accessory. Days with events will be circled on the Monthly Calendar.

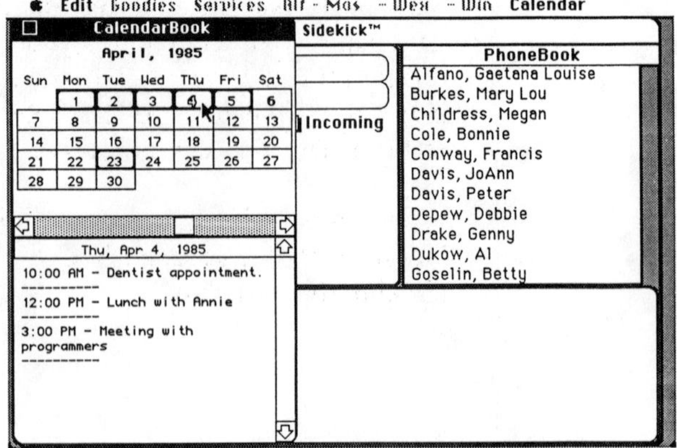

Week-at-a-Peek

Week-at-a-Peek is available from the **Calendar** pull-down menu while displaying the Monthly Calendar.

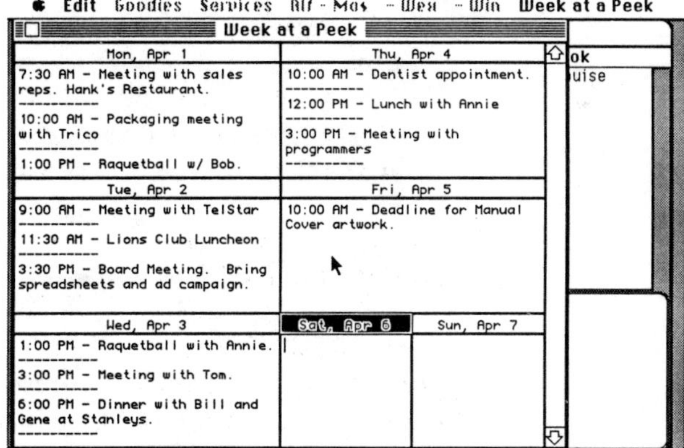

Days of the week are clicked and information entered. Automatic word-wrap allows you to type rapidly without concern for margins. Pressing Return delineates each entry. Search features for any selected day are available in the Week-at-a-Peek pull-down menu.

Week-at-a-Peek can be printed using Traveling SideKick for the Macintosh. Close Week-at-a-Peek by clicking the close box.

SideKick Accessories

Your SideKick application disk has all of SideKick's accessories installed in the **Apple** pull-down menu. These programs can be installed onto other application disks using SideKick's Desk Accessory Installer. The procedure for installing accessories is covered in *Installing SideKick's Accessories*. This section of *Fast Track* will briefly describe each accessory. Each can be viewed simply by *choosing* the accessory name from the **Apple** pull-down menu while running SideKick's application.

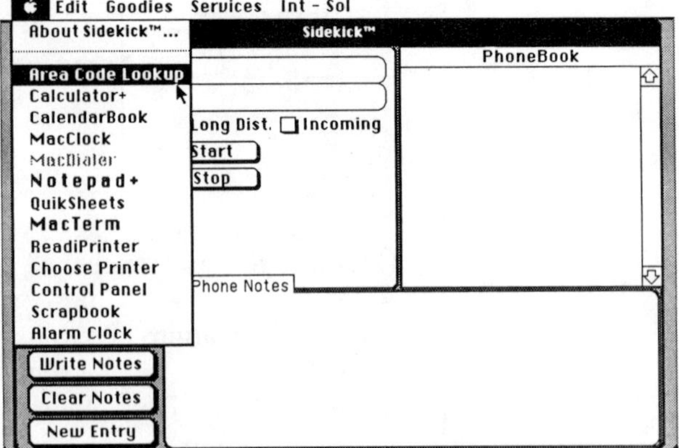

Many accessories have unique pull-down menus that become available after the accessory display is presented. Most accessories have Help screens available as the last command in these menus.

Area Code Lookup

Area Code Lookup will display the *locality, region* and *time-zone* for the entered area code. Simply type in the area code.

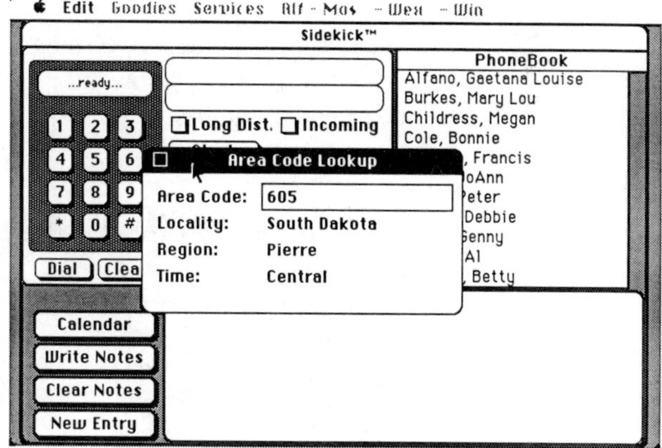

Note: Since the area codes are also stored as a Notepad+text file, you can use Notepad+ search feature to find the area code of a given city.

Calculator+

Calculator+ is a multifunction business calculator that features paper-tape to screen and printer. Values, functions and operations can be entered by clicking the calculator keys, or by typing from the keyboard.

Calculator+ operates like most standard calculators; a number is entered followed by the operation, subsequent number and equal sign.

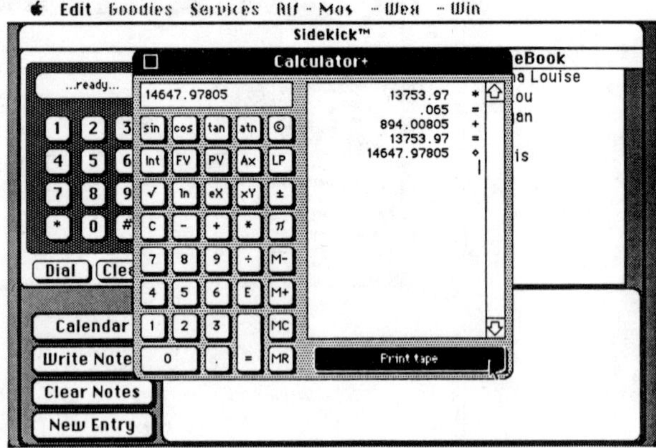

The following is a list of keys, their function and keyboard analog:

Key	Keyboard Analog	Function
sin	s	sine of entered number
cos	c	cosine of entered number
tan	t	tangent of entered number
atn	a	arctangent of entered number
Int	Shift + I	set interest rate for financial functions
FV	Shift + F	future value
PV	Shift + P	present value
Ax	Shift + A	annuity
LP	Shift + L	level payment plan
MR		memory recall
MC		memory clear
M+		memory plus the value displayed
M−		memory minus the value displayed
√‾	Option + v	square root of number entered
ln	l	natural log of number entered
eX	e	the number *e* raised to the x power
xY	x	the variable x raised to the y power
±	Shift + Option + =	change the sign of the number entered
C	Shift + C	clear the last entry
C (twice)	Shift + C (twice)	clear the entire equation
−	−	subtraction
+	Shift + =	addition
*	Shift + 8	multiplication
÷	/	division
Π	Option + p	enter Pi
E	Shift + E	exponential notation (power of 10)
=	= or Enter	equals

MacClock

MacClock is a convenient analog clock with a sweep-second hand. The time settings are regulated by the system clock, which can be adjusted from the control panel.

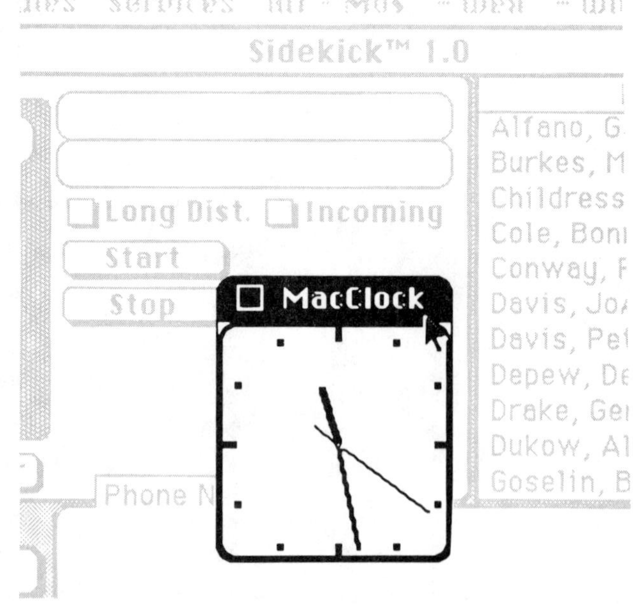

MacDialer

MacDialer is an abbreviated version of the SideKick application program. The MacDialer accessory allows you to automatically dial a number without quitting the application you're currently operating since it's available in the **Apple** menu.

The current MacDialer item of the **Apple** pull-down menu appears shaded since you have the SideKick application opened. To view the accessory, you must quit the SideKick application and choose *MacDialer* from the **Apple** menu at the finder level. Since MacDialer's operations function similarly to the application already discussed, briefly review the display below and move on to the next accessory:

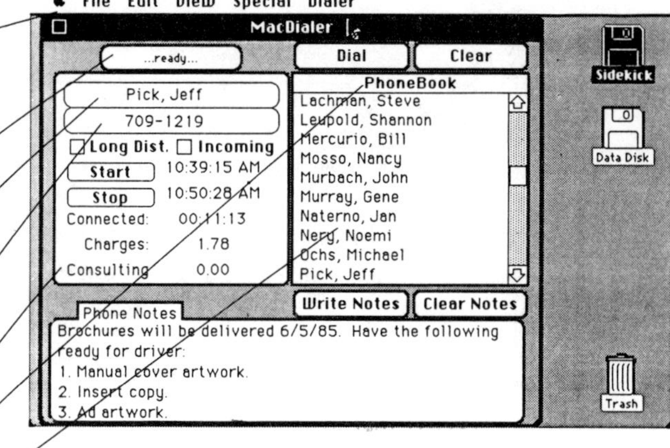

Abbreviated version of SideKick pulldown menus. Notice **Dialer** has been added to the menu bar.

Dialing status window

Active name window

Active number window

Time-stamp and billing

PhoneBook filename

PhoneBook window

Notepad +

Notepad+ is a mini-word processor that creates Macintosh text files compatible with MacWrite™ and Microsoft's Word.™ When you *choose* Notepad+ from the **Apple** menu, a file menu listing all of your Macintosh text files is displayed. Select the file you wish to open, or click **Blank Page** to present a new Notepad+ page.

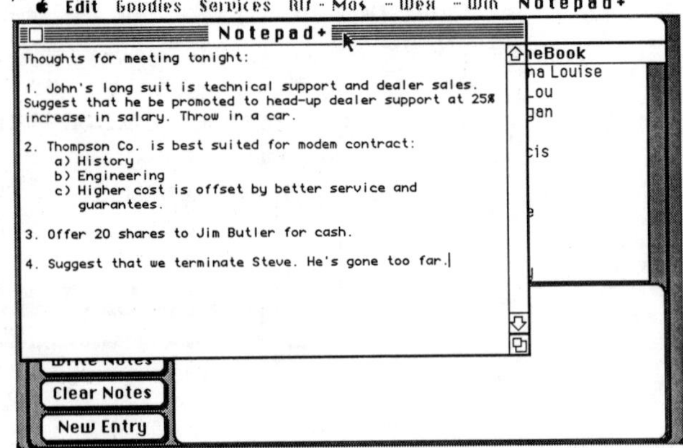

Notepad+'s window is size adjustable (i.e., grow boxes) and movable for convenient placement while running with other applications.

QuikSheets

QuikSheets is a convenient list and record keeper in notepad format. There are four different sheets that make up the pad including Alarms, Expenses, Credit Cards and Things-To-Do. QuikSheets can be printed in pocketbook format with PrintManager. You have the option of printing blank sheets or sheets containing entered data.

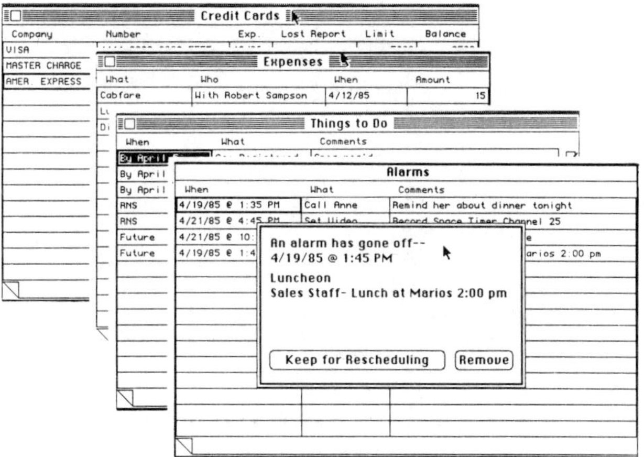

Flip through the QuikSheet pages by clicking the bottom left-hand corner: clicking the turned-up corner presents the next sheet and the flat corner presents the preceding sheet. The *Squeeze the list* command of the **QuikSheets** menu allows you to remove past alarms, things that have been done (checked-off items) or blank lines. All sheets can be saved as text files.

MacTerm

MacTerm is SideKick's terminal program used to operate 300, 1200 and 2400 baud, Hayes compatible modems. Before using MacTerm, you must establish certain communication parameters with the Configure MacTerm utility found on the finder. Once the configuration is established, MacTerm is ready to be installed and operate behind any Macintosh program. (Refer to Configure MacTerm on page 114).

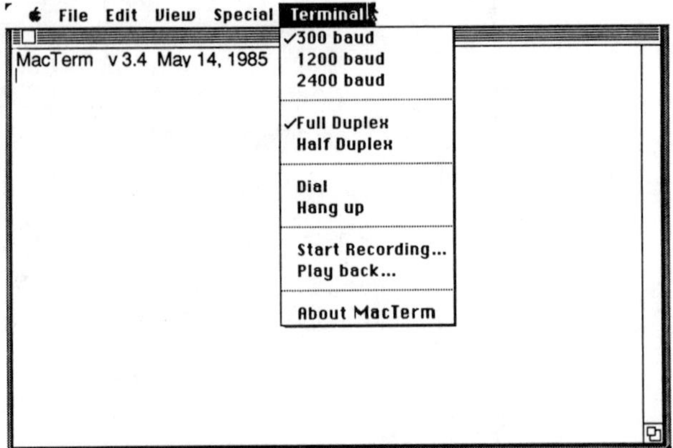

Features of MacTerm include:

1. Automatic dialing from a directory for commonly used numbers.

2. Integration with Notepad+ for sending and capturing data.

Operating QuikTerm:

1. Dial a carrier from the MacTerm directory (choose *Dial* from **Terminal** menu) or manually using the AT command set. "OK" signifies proper carrier detect.

2. Choose *Playback...* and select the text file you wish to transmit.

3. For capturing data, choose *Start Recording...* . The data will be saved as a Notepad+ text file.

ReadiPrinter

ReadiPrinter is a software spooling program designed to print any Macintosh text file without tying up your Mac. Choosing *ReadiPrinter* from the **Apple** menu presents a text file menu for you to select the file for printing. After a file is selected, and the **Print** button clicked, a dialogue box is displayed for you to format the print-out.

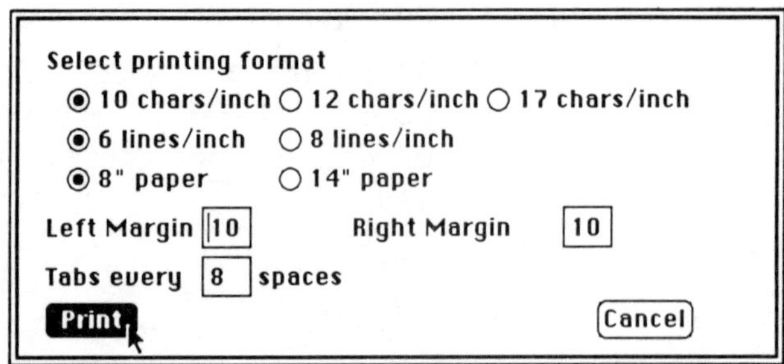

Since "Tab" keys are registered as an ASCII character, each Tab will produce the number of spaces designated in the ***Tabs every*** □ ***spaces*** field. This is a convenient way of indenting or listing columns in any text file.

Once the format is established, click the **Print** button.

To cancel the print-out click ReadiPrinter's close box.

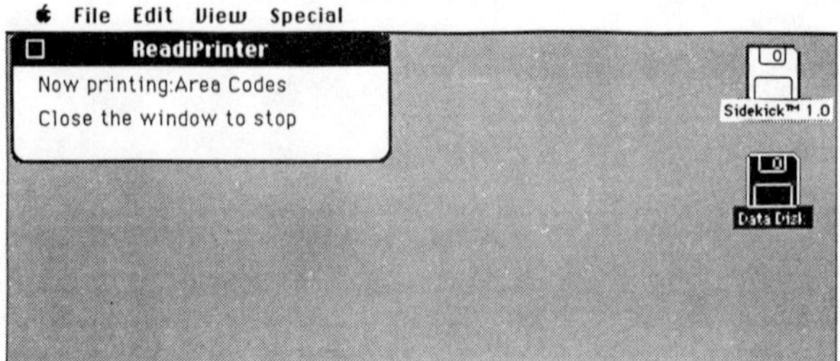

SIDEKICK APPLICATION

The SideKick application is the core of the SideKick package. It is here where you have unlimited access to the PhoneBook files, plus a complete set of telephone management and PhoneLog features. It is also your means for creating new PhoneBooks. PhoneBooks created with the SideKick application, can be accessed while operating the "background" accessory, MacDialer, behind other applications.

Since all of SideKick's accessories are always available while running the SideKick application, you are one click away from all of SideKick's utility; either from the Apple pull-down menu or from the main display's buttons and windows.

This chapter explains how to operate SideKick as an application. From this discussion you will learn how to use the various utilities that make up the main display. The following chapter will describe the use of the accessories available in the Apple pull-down menu.

Note: A series of ***Help*** *screens for operating SideKick's applications are available by choosing* ***About SideKick*** *from the* ***Apple*** *pull-down menu.*

With the SideKick disk desktop opened:

■ **Double-click the SideKick icon to bring up the SideKick application.**

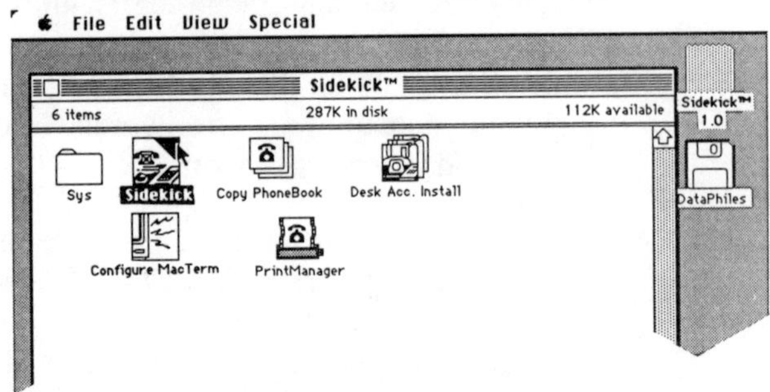

SideKick Main Display

The SideKick main display allows you to access all SideKick operations—either from the Apple pull-down menu or from the main display's buttons, windows and pull-down menus. Take time to explore the features of this display:

Edit pull-down menu is used to Cut, Copy and Paste information to other Macintosh applications and accessories.

Services pull-down menu is used for entering long distance services.

PhoneBook pull-down menu is used for entering long distance services.

Goodies pull-down menu is used for a variety of telephone operations.
The important items include:
Log Calls—if checked will record all calls to the PhoneLog after clicking the **Stop** button for each call.
Sort by Name or by Category—displays the PhoneBook alphabetically by name or category.
Change Area Code—designate your particular area code.
Examine PhoneLog—brings up the PhoneLog window.
Change PhoneBooks—presents a file menu of your PhoneBooks for you to choose for display.

Long Distance box is used to select or deselect the use of the long distance service checked-off in the **Services** pull-down menu.

Incoming box is used to designate a call as incoming. If checked, the call will be logged as [in] and phone charges will not be calculated.

Active name window—tells you who you're calling.

Time-stamp and billing displayed here.

PhoneBook filename listed here. PhoneBooks can be changed from the **Goodies** pull-down menu.

Active number window—tells you the number that is being dialed.

Dialing status window—tells you when to pick-up the phone, etc.

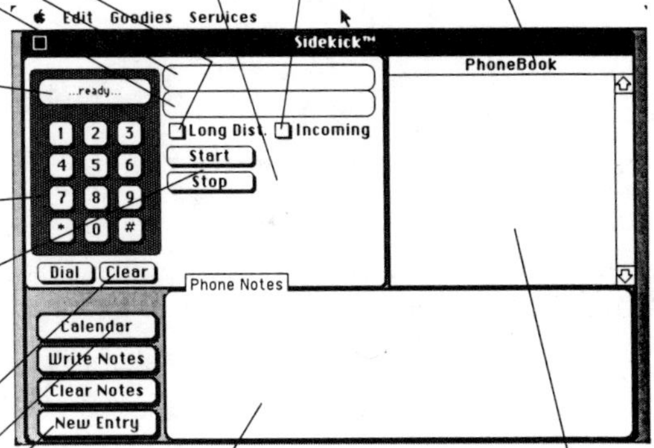

Manual dialing pad—clicking these buttons will generate dial tones.

Start and **Stop** button are used to accurately time the call. Clicking the Stop button will rcord the call to the PhoneLog.

Clear is used to clear the active name and number windows.

Calendar is used to bring up the monthly Calendarbook or Week-at-a-Peek.

New Entry is used to enter new names into the current PhoneBook.

Phone Notes is always available for jotting down notes about a call. Clicking the **Write Notes** button will append the notes to the PhoneLog. **Clear Notes** will clear the Phone Notes window.

PhoneBook window will display all entries in the selected PhoneBook. It can be viewed alphabetically by *name* or by *category* as selected from the **Goodies** pull-down menu. Names may be selected for dialing here: Click the name and then the **Dial** button. Information about the person you're calling is temporarily displayed in the PhoneBook window.

Another source of utility is the **Apple** pull-down menu.

■ **Click and hold the Apple pull-down menu.**

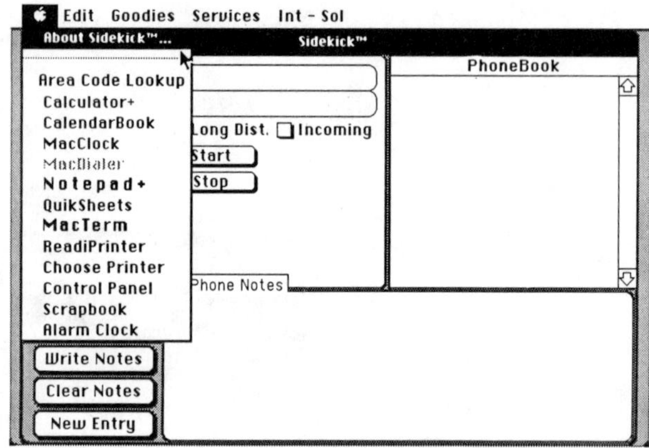

Never before has this menu appeared so useful. All SideKick accessories reside in this menu and are available when you run SideKick as an application.. Feel free to *choose* any that you wish. Note that the MacDialer accessory is shaded (and therefore inaccessible) since the SideKick application with all of MacDialer's features is currently operating. Put away all opened accessories by clicking the close box at the top left corner of each window. How to use each accessory will be discussed in a later chapter.

Become familiar with the pull-down menus that make up the main display. Begin with the **Edit** menu which is used for editing many of SideKick's utilities:

■ **Click and hold the Edit pull-down menu.**

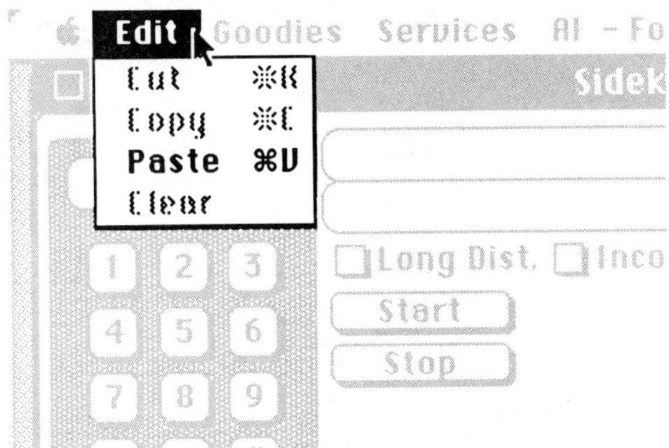

SideKick applications and accessories utilize the primary clipboard for Cut, Copy and Paste operations. This edit feature provides a convenient way of transferring information between accessories and applications.

The next menu is named **Goodies** and contains a number of different commands for your telephone operations:

■ **Click and hold the Goodies pull-down menu.**

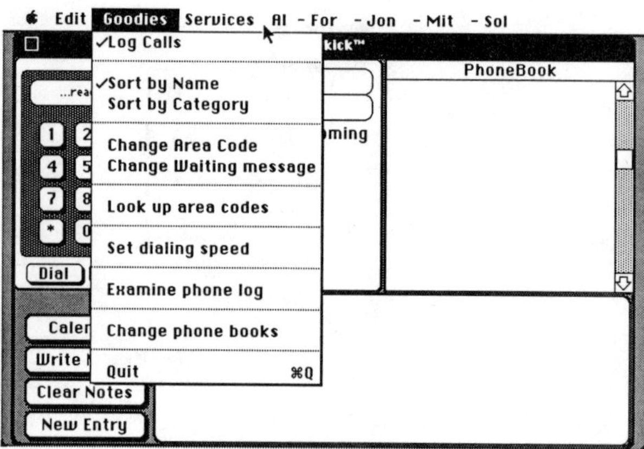

Log Calls—used to record phone activities in the phone log.

Sort by Name—Used to sort the current PhoneBook alphabetically by name.
Sort by Category—Used to sort the current PhoneBook alphabetically by category.

Change Area Code—Used to designate your particular area code. If the area code of a dialed number is different from yours, the area code will be preceded by a "1".

Change Waiting Message—Used to create a custom waiting message in the dialing status window.

Look Up Area Codes—Used to determine the locality and time zone of a particular area code.

Set Dialing Speed—Used to adjust the rate of dialing tone output. *Choosing* this command presents a speed adjusting scroll bar.

Examine PhoneLog—Used to display the PhoneLog and the PhoneLog pull-down menu.

Change PhoneBooks—Used to change the PhoneBook currently displayed. *Choosing* this command presents a file menu listing all of the available PhoneBook files. Buttons are present for changing drives or disks. To select a PhoneBook, click to highlight the filename and then click the **Open** button. The selected PhoneBook will appear in the PhoneBook window.

Quit—Used to quit the SideKick application.

The next menu is named **Services.**

■ **Click and hold the Services pull-down menu.**

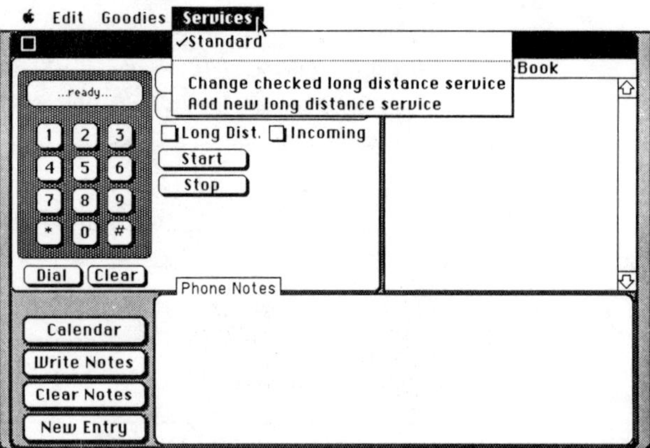

This menu is used to select a particular long distance or credit card service that you want to use. The service that is checked is the one used if the *"use long distance service"* box is checked in the PhoneBook files. The default service is *standard* for calls using conventional phone lines.

The remaining pull-down menus are reserved for selected PhoneBook entries that you most frequently call. There are potentially four menus, each containing twenty entries. The first and last entry of each menu are abbreviated in the menu bar for easy reference. By choosing a name from the PhoneBook menu, the telephone number will automatically be dialed and the call timed.

Before entering names into the PhoneBook files, you must inform SideKick of your particular area code so it knows which calls are long distance and which are local.

- **Choose *Change Area Code* from the Goodies pull-down menu.**
- **Enter your area code. Press RETURN (or click the OK button).**

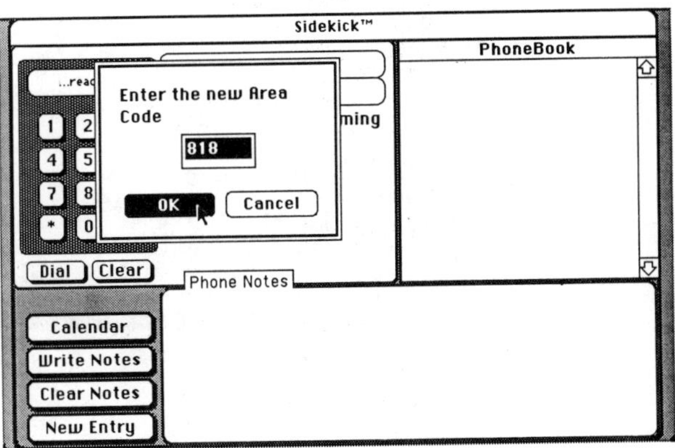

SideKick is now customized for your locality. If the area code of the number being called (entered on the index card) is not the same as yours, SideKick will recognize that the call is not local and automatically precede the area code with "1."

PhoneBook Files

To make an entry into the PhoneBook Files:

■ **Click the New Entry button at the bottom left corner of the main display. A blank index card will be presented.**

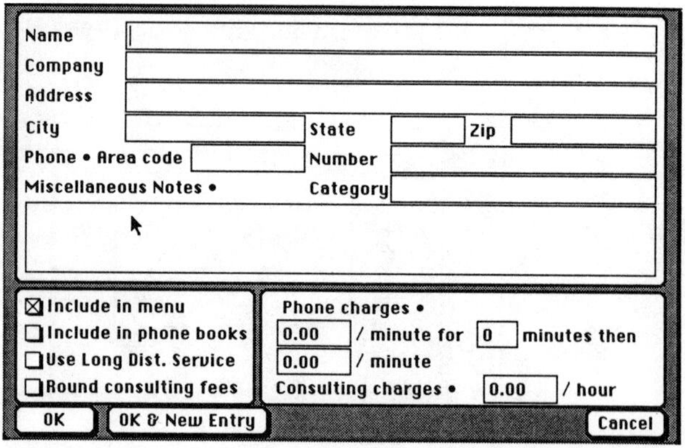

Name
Company
Address
City State Zip
Phone • Area code Number
Miscellaneous Notes • Category

☒ Include in menu
☐ Include in phone books
☐ Use Long Dist. Service
☐ Round consulting fees

Phone charges •
0.00 / minute for 0 minutes then
0.00 / minute
Consulting charges • 0.00 / hour

OK | OK & New Entry | Cancel

The information entered on these cards is used as the "database" for SideKick. The PhoneBook pull-down menus will alphabetically display the first eighty entries with the *include in menu* field checked on the index cards. By choosing a name from the PhoneBook pull-down menu, you can automatically dial that person's phone number.

The PhoneBook window displays all of the names included in the PhoneBook files. This window is scrollable and virtually unlimited in the number of names it can hold. Names are displayed in the PhoneBook window alphabetically either by name, or by category. When a name in the PhoneBook window is clicked, the phone number is displayed in the dialer activity window, and the personal data about the person you're calling is temporarily presented in the PhoneBook window. To automatically dial the number, simply click the **Dial** button.

To illustrate the SideKick telephone dialing and management capabilities, fill out the blank personal index card displayed on your screen:

- **Type the *Name* of the person, last name first. Press Tab.**
- **Type the *Company* or another appropriate reference. Press Tab.**
- **Type the street *Address*. Press Tab.**
- **Type the *City*. Press Tab.**
- **Type the *State*. Press Tab.**
- **Type the *Zip* code. Press Tab.**
- **Type the *Area code*. Press Tab.**
- **Type the *Phone number*. Press Tab.**

The blinking cursor appears in the *Category* field. Since this field can be used to sort the PhoneBook from either the application or accessory, be selective with the name you choose for *Category.* Some good examples of category names include: students, printers, typists, etc. Abbreviations may be required since there's a limit to nine characters.

When sorted by the *Category* field (available from the **Goodies** pull-down menu), the PhoneBook window will display the list alphabetically by *Category.*

■ **Type a *Category* name. Press Tab.**

The blinking cursor now appears in the *Misc. Notes* field. This field is reserved for any information you wish to associate with the person, such as personal data or business relationship.

■ **Type in a *Misc. Note.* Press Tab.**

The cursor will blink in the *Phone Charges* field.The billing information must be entered in this field if you want SideKick to compute the cost when calling this telephone number. Refer to your telephone directory or contact your local telephone company for the current billing rates.

■ **Type in the appropriate billing rates. Press Tab.**

The cursor now appears in the *Consultation Charges* field. If you plan to charge this person for professional services over the telephone, enter your rate into this field.

- **Type in the appropriate consultation rate. Press RETURN.**
- **If you bill by fifteen minute increments, click the *Round consulting fees* box.**
- **If you wish to include this name in the pull-down menu, click the box labeled *Include in menus*.**
- **If you wish to include this name when making copies of your PhoneBook (explained in chapter, Copy PhoneBook), click the box labeled *Include in phonebooks.***
- **If you want to use a long-distance service when calling this number, click the box labeled *Use long distance service.***

If the data you've entered is accurate:

- **Click the OK button**

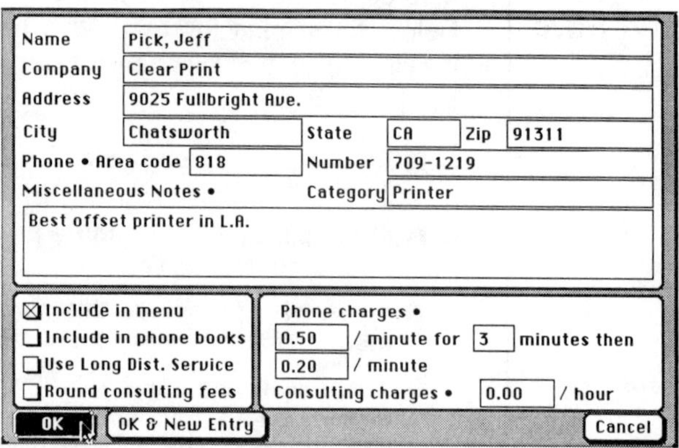

The information will be recorded in the PhoneBook data file and you will return to the main display. Notice that the new entry has been added to the PhoneBook window.

Include as many names in the PhoneBook as you wish. You may add, edit or delete an entry at any time. To add an entry, click the **New Entry** button.

To edit or delete an entry, double-click the name in the PhoneBook window to bring up the personal index card. Edit any field by pointing to it and double-clicking. When highlighted, type in the new information. To delete the name entirely, click the **Delete** button. A dialog box will verify your intentions. To present the next PhoneBook entry card, click the **OK and Next** button.

Copy and Save

It may be convenient to use the **Copy and Save** button for those personal index cards which share similar information. For instance, if your PhoneBook is to include a group of people from the same company, record the first completed entry into the PhoneBook by clicking the **OK** button. When the main display is presented, locate and double-click the new entry listed in the PhoneBook window to present the index card. The card is displayed this time with a **Copy and Save** button used to make a duplicate PhoneBook entry.

■ **Click the Copy and Save button.**

The main display will be presented with the duplicate entry registered in the PhoneBook window.

■ **Double-click one of the duplicate entries in the PhoneBook window.**

The duplicate index card is presented. Edit the *Name* and *Misc. Notes* fields accordingly.

PhoneLink

To use the dialing capabilities of SideKick, you must have the PhoneLink interface cable connected from the audio output port of your Macintosh to the handset modular jack on your telephone. Be sure to carefully follow the instructions in the PhoneLink installation guide.

Placing a Telephone Call

When you have posted at least one entry into the PhoneBook, you can use SideKick to dial the number for you automatically. The following steps illustrate how simple it is to dial:

- **Point to the name of the person listed in the PhoneBook window you wish to call and click.**

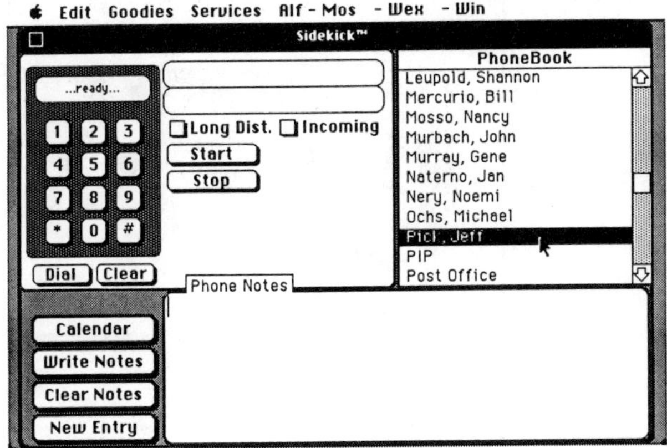

When you click a name in the PhoneBook window, several things happen:

1. The name will become highlighted.
2. Information about the person will be momentarily displayed in the PhoneBook window.
3. The name selected will be listed in the "name" window.
4. The phone number to be dialed will be listed in the "number" window.
5. If the index card is checked for long distance service, an "X" will appear in the "Long Dist." box.

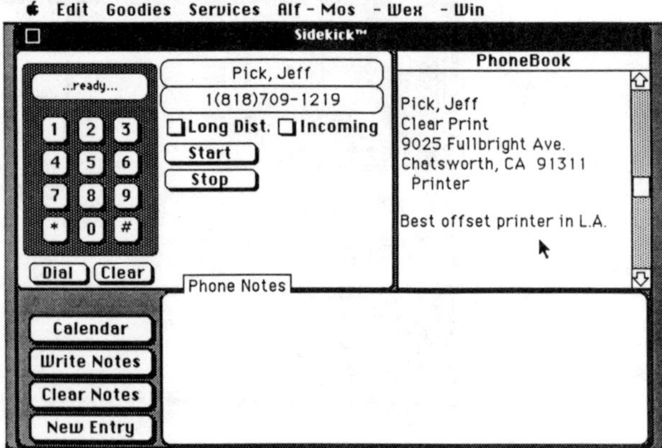

- **Point to the Dial button and click.**

The dialer activity window will prompt you to "Pick up phone."

- **Pick up the handset and listen.**

SideKick immediately dials the telephone number selected. You will be able to hear the tones as the call is being placed.

The word "Online" appears in the activity window to indicate that the numbers are being dialed and the call is being timed.

*Note: SideKick will place the call **only** if you pick up the handset. You must pick up the phone immediately when prompted. If the number is not dialed correctly, hang up the phone, click **Dial** to redial the number, and pick up the handset when prompted. If the number is not dialed correctly again, adjust the dialing speed from the **Goodies** pull-down menu. If the number is dialed correctly this time, reset the starting time by clicking the **Start** button.*

If you get a "busy" signal when making a call, click the **Clear** button and try again later.

Pull-Down Menus

There is an even faster way to make a phone call with SideKick. As mentioned earlier, the top right half of the pull-down menu bar is reserved for names included in the PhoneBook pull-down menus. There are potentially four menus, each containing twenty names. Use these menus to list the people you most frequently call. To be included, a name must have the *Include in menus* box checked on their personal index card.

The names in the pull-down menus are arranged alphabetically in columns from left to right. The first three characters of the first and last entry in each column are listed at the top to help you find names quickly.

Dialing from the menus is a one-click operation. Simply *choose* the name you wish to call.

- **Choose a name from the pull-down menu.**

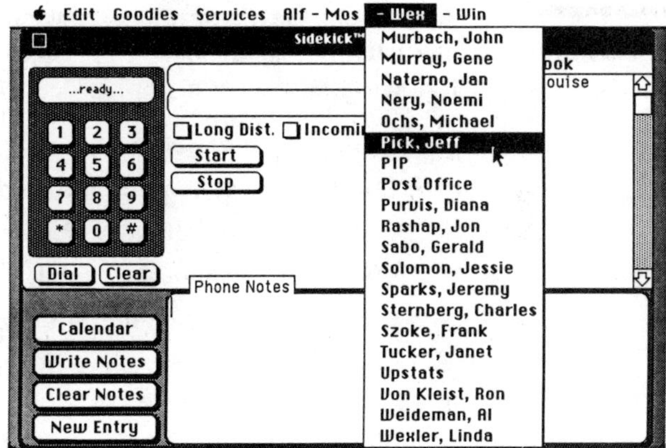

The dialing activity window will change from "Ready" to "Pick up phone" to "Online" just as with the Dial button method.

- **Pick up the handset and listen. If the line is open and the dial speed setting is adjusted properly, the call will go through.**

Active Display

After a call has been made, several bits of information are actively displayed. On the SideKick display, the following information is recorded:

- ☐ **Starting time of call.**
- ☐ **Current time continually updated.**
- ☐ **Connect time continually updated.**
- ☐ **Cost of call continually updated.**
- ☐ **Consulting fees continually updated.**

About the Buttons

Dial is used to dial the number displayed in the active number window.

Clear is used to clear all active displays.

Start is used to reset the starting time for misdials, long ring times, etc. Clicking this button will update the starting time for connect time and charges.

Stop is used to stop the connect time and consultation charges. It also acts as a Hold button—once clicked, it converts to **Resume**. If clicked, the **Resume** button will resume connect time and consultation fees, and update the connect time (since you're still connected and being charged for the call while on hold).

*Note: Each time you click the **Stop** button, the call (or a portion of the call) is automatically recorded to the PhoneLog. If a call is not connected, click **Clear** so the call is not recorded to the log.*

Phone Notes

You probably have noticed a note pad at the bottom of the display. The Phone Notes window is a convenient place to jot down any notes about the call. These notes can be appended to the PhoneLog entry by clicking the **Write Notes** button. They also may be cut and pasted to the Calendar, Notepad+ or any other SideKick accessory. To enter a Phone Note:

- **Type in any pertinent information about the telephone conversation.**

To append the notes to the call recorded in the PhoneLog:

- **Click the Write Notes button.**
- **Click the Stop button**

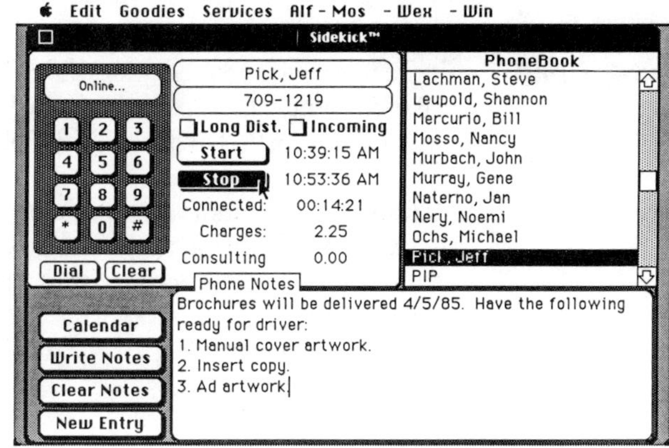

To clear the Phone Notes pad for future calls:

- **Click the Clear Notes button.**

It's important to clear the note pad after each call. If not cleared, the note entered will be recorded for each subsequent call.

Note: You can also store a note on the PhoneLog even when you're NOT using the telephone. Simply type the note in the Phone Notes window and click the ***Write Notes*** *button. Your note will appear in the PhoneLog after the last call placed. Be sure to* ***Clear Notes*** *afterwards.*

Incoming Calls

SideKick is capable of logging information for incoming calls simply by clicking the "Incoming" box on the display. When the box is checked, the PhoneLog entry will be designated with an [in] (incoming).

The time and duration of the call will also be recorded to the log if the **Start** and **Stop** buttons are clicked. Note the charges remain at zero since it's an incoming call.

The name of the person calling *in* can be recorded in one of two ways:

1. If the caller is listed in the PhoneBook, simply point to and click the name in the PhoneBook window. The name will appear in the active name window. If professional fees are to be billed, the charges will accrue in the Consulting field after clicking the **Start** button (if the rate is entered on the personal index card).
2. If the caller is not listed in the PhoneBook, point to the active name window, click and type in the name. You may also want to record the caller's phone number for future reference. Simply press Tab to enter the active number window and type in the phone number.

Using Long Distance and Credit Card Services

SideKick accomodates the use of long distance services. The access and authorization numbers for as many as five different services can be entered into the **Services** pull-down menu. To enter a long distance number:

- **Point to the Services pull-down menu and choose *Add new long distance service.***

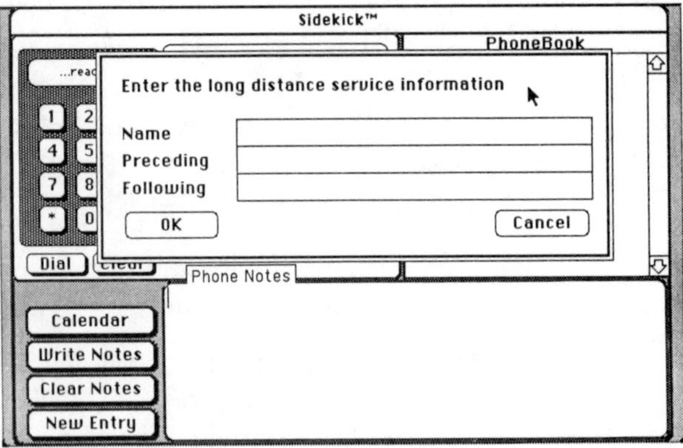

- **Point to the Services pull-down menu and choose *Add new long distance service.***

A window will appear for you to enter the long distance service information.

- **Type in the name of the service. Press Tab.**

The cursor moves to the *Preceding* field. When the *Use long distance service* is selected (on the personal index card), the number entered in this field will be dialed before the area code and phone number.

- **Type in the access, authorization and local number for the service.**
- **Press RETURN.**

Note: Certain long distance services (such as MCI) require a pause before your authorization code is entered. You can use the ampersand (&) or plus (+) symbols for pauses. Each "&" creates a one-second pause while each "+" creates a ten-second pause. For example:

5551212&&&&&&&&&&87654

and

5551212+87654

would both give you a ten-second pause between the telephone number and your access code. You can easily determine the length of the pause needed by timing a "test call" to your service.

The *Following* field can be used for any numbers you need to dial *following* the telephone number. This suffix field can be used for credit card numbers

- **Enter the number (plus any necessary pauses) and press Tab.**

Note: If Services is used for a credit card number, enter a zero (0) in the Preceding field and the credit card number in the Following field. Title the service appropriately (i.e., Credit Card). If the long distance service box is checked and the Credit Card option selected, the credit card number will be automatically dialed.

After completing the Services entry:

■ **Click the OK button.**

The name of the service is presented in the **Services** pull-down menu. Follow this procedure to include additional long distance or credit card services.

To edit an existing service entry, *choose* the service from the **Services** pull-down menu to show it as checked or "selected." Choose *Change checked long distance service* to present the entry window. Modify the fields with standard editing techniques and save the changes by clicking the **OK** button.

SideKick will automatically include these numbers during the dialing sequence as long as the *Use long distance service* box is checked on the index card for the person being called (in which case, the *long distance box* on the dialer display will also be checked). The particular carrier to be used is the one selected in the *Services* pull-down menu.

You can bypass the use of a long distance service (for numbers which have *Use long distance service* selected on the Phonebook index card) by clicking the *Long Dist.* box on the dialer display. This will delete the "X" and the long distance service will not be used.

Note: Removing the "X" from the dialer display will not affect the long distance indication on the personal index card. If you uncheck long distance from the dialer display, you must enter "1" before the area code of the phone number displayed in the active number window.

To uncheck long distance service from the dialer display and dial:

- **Point to the Long Dist. box and click. The "X" will be removed.**
- **Point to the left of the phone number listed in the active number window and click. An editing cursor appears.**
- **Type 1.**
- **Click the Dial button.**

The number will be dialed without the use of a long distance service.

Local Calls With A Different Area Code

Many large cities have more than one area code within a "local-call" region. These calls are not considered long distance and do not require a "1" preceding the area code. Since SideKick automatically enters a "1" for any number with an area code different from yours, you must create and use a "long distance service" with a blank *Preceding* field. This will eliminate the "1" preceding the area code.

- **Choose *Add new long distance service* from the Services pull down menu.**

The information window will appear.

- **Enter "Local" in the *name* field. Press Return and click the OK button.**

To call local numbers with a different area code:

- **Check the Use Long Dist. Service box on the PhoneBook index card for numbers that do not require a "1" before the area code.**
- **Choose *Local* from the Services pull-down menu before making the call.**

The number will be dialed without "1" preceding the area code.

PhoneLog

SideKick's PhoneLog will provide you with a complete record of your telephone activities. This information is automatically logged when you click the **Stop** button at the end of each call. To view the recorded information:

- **Choose *Examine PhoneLog* from the Goodies pull-down menu.**

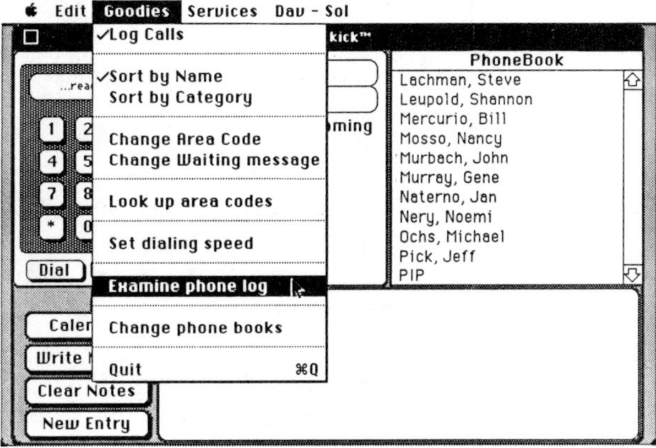

The PhoneLog window will appear. As the column labels indicate, the logged information includes: the ***Phone Number*** dialed, the ***Name*** of the person called, ***Start*** and ***Stop*** times, ***Duration*** of call, ***Phone Charges***, ***Consulting Fees***, and ***Date***.

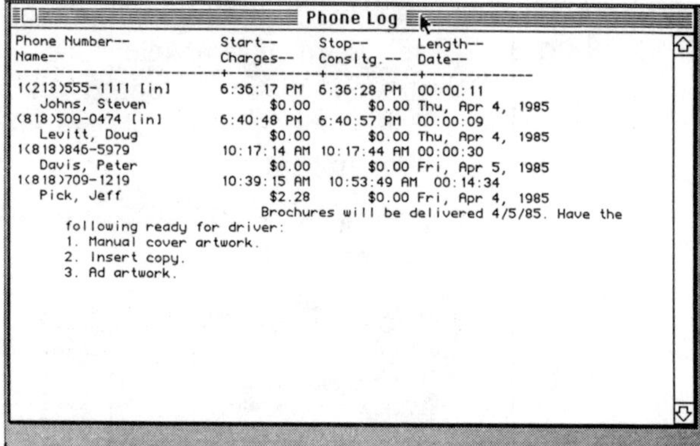

Edit Phone Log
Phone Log
Phone Number-- Start-- Stop-- Length--
Name-- Charges-- Conslt.-- Date--
1(213)555-1111 [in] 6:36:17 PM 6:36:28 PM 00:00:11
Johns, Steven $0.00 $0.00 Thu, Apr 4, 1985
(818)509-0474 [in] 6:40:48 PM 6:40:57 PM 00:00:09
Levitt, Doug $0.00 $0.00 Thu, Apr 4, 1985
1(818)846-5979 10:17:14 AM 10:17:44 AM 00:00:30
Davis, Peter $0.00 $0.00 Fri, Apr 5, 1985
1(818)709-1219 10:39:15 AM 10:53:49 AM 00:14:34
Pick, Jeff $2.28 $0.00 Fri, Apr 4, 1985
Brochures will be delivered 4/5/85. Have the
following ready for driver:
1. Manual cover artwork.
2. Insert copy.
3. Ad artwork.

The PhoneLog also shows whether the call was incoming or was made using a long distance service. In addition, any Phone Notes "written" to the log will be appended to the call.

Note that the PhoneLog window has its own set of pull-down menus. The Edit menu allows you to modify the current phone log before printing a hard copy. The PhoneLog menu has a complete set of commands and options:

- **Point to the PhoneLog pull-down menu, click and hold.**

The PhoneLog menu offers the following commands:

Sort by name—Converts the chronological list of calls to an alphabetical list

---

Remove all incoming calls—Deletes all incoming [in] calls from the log

Remove all local calls—Deletes all calls that are not labeled "L.D." from the log

---

Clear the log—Clears the PhoneLog display. The previous log may be retrieved by selecting the revert to previous log command.

Print the log—Print a hardcopy of the log.

Save the log back to disk—Used to store the displayed version of the log back to disk. Since there is only one PhoneLog file, executing this command will replace the stored log with whatever is displayed.

Revert to the previous log—Used to replace the displayed log with the version stored on disk. This command is also used to replace a name sort with a chronological sort of the PhoneLog.

The PhoneLog file should be printed and cleared daily to keep SideKick running efficiently. Simply choose *Print the log*, then *Clear the log* after printing a copy. To close the PhoneLog window, click the close box at the top left-hand corner.

CalendarBook

The utility of SideKick becomes clear when the time management features of the CalendarBook are combined with the phone and information features already discussed. SideKick's CalendarBook allows you, while talking on the telephone, to schedule appointments, and view any month to the year 2030. Weekly schedules can be entered into Week-at-a-Peek and printed in convenient pocketbook form with SideKick's Print-Manager application.

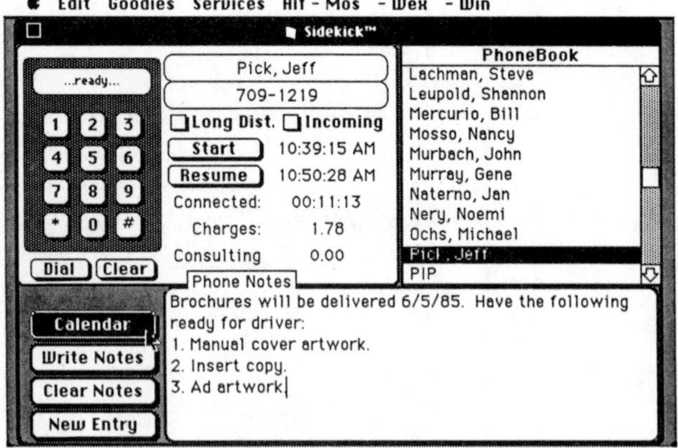

The CalendarBook can be viewed by clicking the Calendar button of the main display. The same CalendarBook is accessed from the **Apple** pull-down menu. In either case, you will be presented with the Monthly Calendar or Week-at-a-Peek, depending on which display the CalendarBook was last closed from.

■ **Click the Calendar button on the main display.**

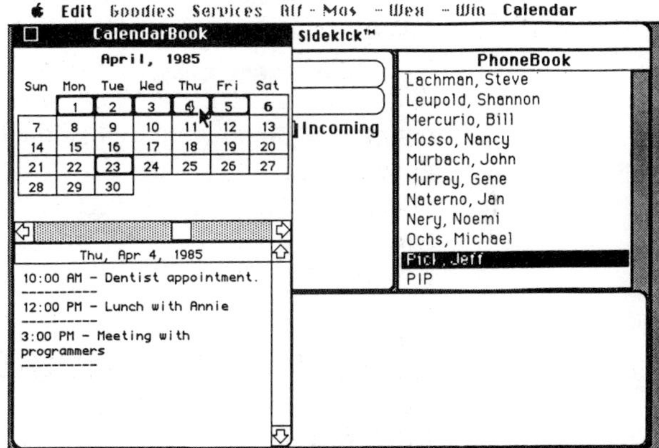

The current month is displayed above a daily notepage. Also note the **Calendar** pull-down menu on the right side of the menu bar. This menu will be present only when the CalendarBook is the front window.

You may change the month displayed by clicking the arrows of the horizontal elevator. To change the year, drag the elevator to the left or right. The CalendarBook dates from January 1905 to December 2030. As an exercise, find the day of your birth:

- **Click, hold, drag and release the horizontal elevator a small distance to the left for coarse adjustment of the year. If you have gone beyond the year of your birth, move the elevator to the right. You may also adjust the calendar yearly by clicking the elevator *shaft* to the right and left of the elevator. Click the shaft until you have the correct year displayed.**

- **Click the arrows to arrive at the month of your birth.**
- **Point to the day of your birth on the monthly calendar and click.**

The daily notepage will show the day you've selected. You may want to type a short memo noting the event. To return quickly to the present:

- **Choose *Jump to current month* from the pull-down menu.**

The information entered will be automatically saved and the current month will be displayed.

To update the daily notepage:

- **Click the current date on the monthly calendar.**
- **Type in a note for today.**

The preceding exercise illustrates how easy it is to select a date from the CalendarBook and enter a memo. Once a daily memo is entered on the notepage, the date is circled on the monthly calendar. The date which has its memo pad displayed at the bottom of the CalendarBook is outlined in the monthly calendar. The current date is displayed in boldface. (If today's notes are being shown, the outline will take precedence.)

Daily notes, memos and appointments can be entered into the *free-form* notepage by typing from the keyboard. SideKick's CalendarBook editing features are found in the **Edit** pull-down menu. You may edit the notes in the standard Macintosh manner—cursor selections are made with the mouse, the scroll bar is used to set the portion of notepage displayed in the window, and so forth. Editing operations utilize the Macintosh clipboard, so you may Cut, Copy and Paste to other accessories and applications.

As you type in a note, the automatic wrap-around will continue the sentence on the next line. When the note is completed, pressing Return will draw a dotted line to separate each note. If one day's set of notes exceeds the size of the window, a scroll bar is available.

The **Calendar** pull-down menu provides a command for word searching the current notepage. This feature is ideal for quickly identifying key appointments for any given day. Searches disregard word breaks or capitalization. The search commands are:

Find: will ask which characters to search for

Same: will use the last set of characters given for the Find command

The search words appear highlighted on the notepage.

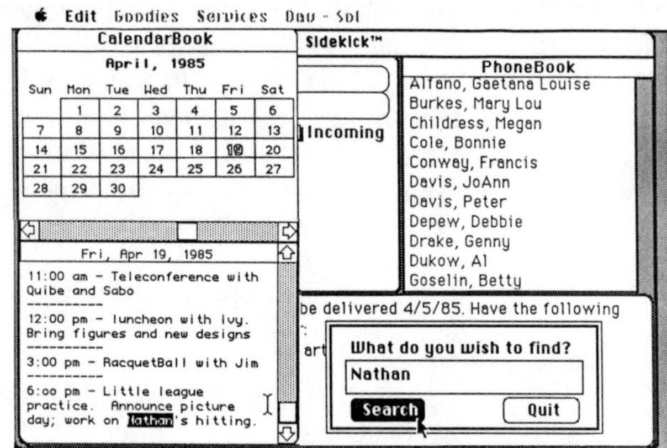

The ***Print*** command of the ***Calendar*** pull-down menu will provide you with a hard copy of the displayed day's notepage.

Updating Calendar Dates

Any changes made to a day's notepage are automatically saved to the Calendar File on your data disk when changing notepages or closing Calendarbook.

To free your calendar of clutter, SideKick automatically "looks" at the Calendar File during start-up. If it finds entries dated past two weeks, you are asked to remove the old entries. If you click the **OK** button, the old notepages will copied into the text file called "Past Memos" and deleted from the CalendarBook. These text files can always be viewed with Macwrite or Notepad+ (SideKick's accessory), or printed with ReadiPrinter. If you select **Cancel**, the past notepages will remain in the CalendarBook file. Be sure to take advantage of this start-up "house cleaning" feature to keep your SideKick running efficiently.

Week-at-a-Peek

One of SideKick's most useful features is Week-at-a-Peek—a seven-day calendar used for scheduling appointments and noting important events. Week-at-a-Peek shares the same calendar file as CalendarBook, so information entered into one is automatically recorded in the other.

The Week-at-a-Peek window is available as a command in the **Calendar** pull-down menu of the CalendarBook accessory:

■ **Choose Week-at-a-Peek from the Calendar pull-down menu.**

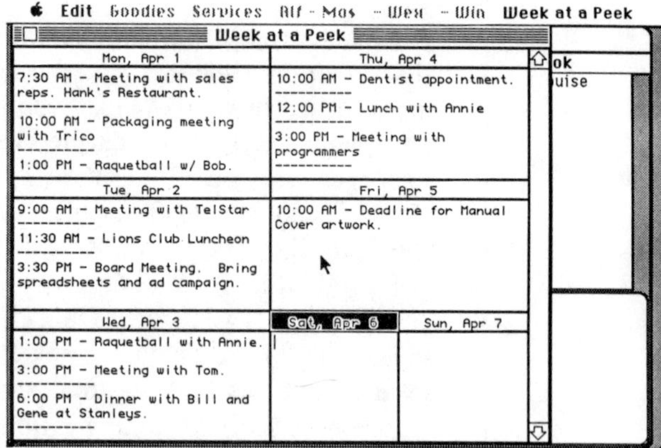

Appointments are typed into Week-a-a-Peek in the same manner as CalendarBook's *free-form* daily notepage. Simply click the day you want to schedule and type. The automatic wrap-around feature will continue the sentence on the next line; pressing Return will delineate each entry. If one day's notes exceed the size of the window, a scroll bar is available for that day.

Week-at-a-Peek has a unique pull-down menu which offers several useful commands:

■ **Point to the *Week-at-a-Peek* pull-down menu, click and hold to view the commands**

This Week, Next Week and ***Last Week*** are options used to select the week displayed in the Week-at-a-Peek window. The option checked corresponds to the week currently displayed.

Find... is a search feature used to find key words for isolating appointments or events for the highlighted day. Selecting this command will present a dialogue box asking for the word you wish to find. Type in the word and click the **Search** button to begin the search. The search words appear highlighted on the notepage.

Same... will use the last set of characters given for the Find command.

Print... will provide you with a hard copy of the displayed week.

Note: Week-at-a-Peek and Year-at-a-Glance may be printed in Pocketbook format with the PrintManager application available on SideKick's desktop. You also have the flexibility of printing any calendar week(s) with PrintManager.

Switch to CalendarBook is used to present the Monthly Calendar and daily notepage display.

About Week-at-a-Peek displays a help screen.

There are two possible ways to exit Week-at-a-Peek. If you want to return to the monthly calendar display:

- **Choose *Switch to CalendarBook* from the Week-at-a-Peek pull-down menu.**

You will be presented with the Monthly Calendar and daily notepage display.

If you want to exit the CalendarBook accessory from Week-at-a-Peek, simply click the close box of the Week-at-a-Peek window. You will return to the main display. Next time you *choose* CalendarBook from the **Apple** pull-down menu (or click the Calendar button), you will be presented with the calendar display last closed.

SIDEKICK ACCESSORIES

The SideKick accessories reside in the **Apple** pull-down menu for both the SideKick application and for installed accessories on other Macintosh programs. This menu includes all of the accessories when SideKick is operated as an application. Only those accessories selected for installation with the Desk Accessory Installer will be included as accessories for other programs.

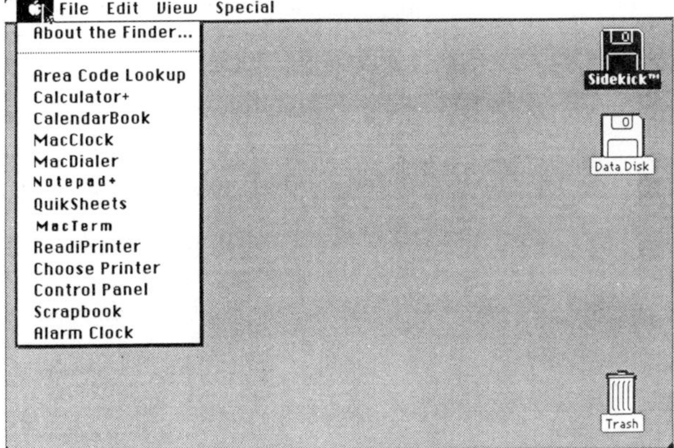

How to operate SideKick's accessories is the subject of this chapter. Installing the accessories *on* and using them *with* other Macintosh programs is the subject of the following chapter. There are no differences between the application accessories and installed accessories.

SideKick offers several important features that are common to most of its accessories. Most notable is SideKick's use of the Macintosh clipboard for editing operations. *Cut, Copy* and *Paste* commands allow you to transfer information between accessories, as well as to other applications.

SideKick's accessories are movable and can overlay one another, thus allowing you to view different displays simultaneously.

Most accessories have a unique pull-down menu that becomes available once the accessory is displayed. The last command of each accessory menu presents a **Help** screen for quick reference.

To view each accessory for this discussion, simply *choose* the appropriate accessory from the **Apple** pull-down menu while using SideKick as a start-up disk. Remain at the finder level.

AREA CODE LOOKUP

Area Code Lookup provides *locality, region* and *time zone* information for all area codes in the North American continent. Simply enter an area code and the information is presented.

The entire list of Area Codes is also available as a text file that can be viewed with Notepad+ and printed by ReadiPrinter.

> *Note: Since the area codes are saved as a text file, you may use the search command while viewing the Area Code file in Notepad+ to find the area code of a particular city.*

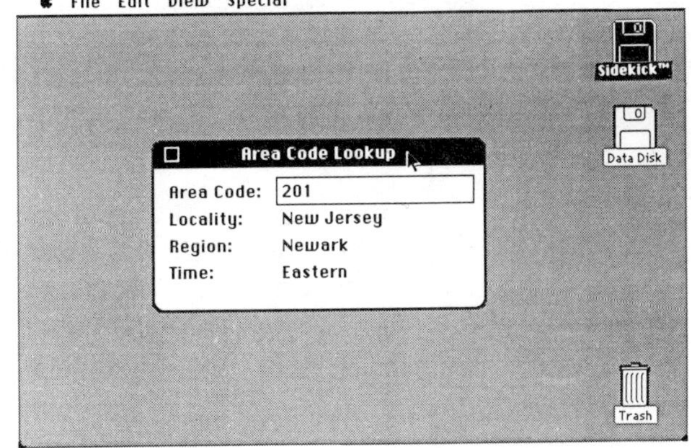

CALCULATOR+

Calculator+ is a multifunction business calculator that features paper-tape to screen and printer. Values, functions and operations can be entered by clicking the keys on the calculator display, or by typing from the keyboard or the Macintosh 10-key pad hardware accessory.

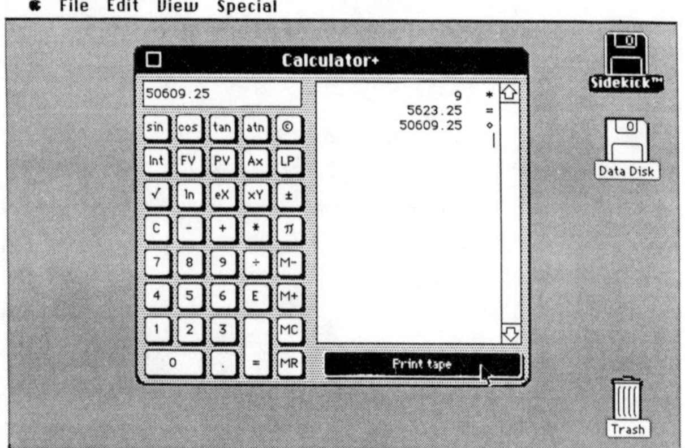

Calculator+ operates like any standard calculator, a number is entered followed by the operation, subsequent number and equal sign: To perform the calculation 8 + 7 =:

- **Click the 8 key.**
- **Click the + key (operation).**

The numeral and operation are copied to the screen-tape.

- **Click the 7 key (addend).**
- **Click the = key (enter equation).**

The addend and equal sign are copied to the screen-tape and the calculation is automatically performed. In this example, 15 is the total as indicated by the diamond on the screen-tape.

Equations are calculated strictly from left to right as the numbers and operations are entered into Calculator+; operations in parentheses or brackets should be performed first. For example, the equation: $(3 \times 4 \times 2 + 6) / 3 \times 10 =$ is entered as follows (note that as you enter the equation, the running total is presented in the calculator window):

- **Click the 3 key.**
- **Click the * key (for multiplication, the * sign is used).**
- **Click the 4 key.**
- **Click the * key.**
- **Click the 2 key.**
- **Click the + key.**
- **Click the 6 key.**
- **Click the ÷ key.**
- **Click the 3 key.**
- **Click the * key.**
- **Click the 1 and 0 keys.**
- **Click the = key.**

A total of 100 is displayed.

Each number and operation is copied to the screen-tape, the running total is displayed in the calculator window and the final total is automatically calculated and displayed on the screen tape. The entries listed on the screen tape can be printed as a hard copy by clicking the **Print tape** button.

Incorrect entries can be cleared by clicking the **C** key. Complete equations already entered are cleared by clicking this same key twice ("Cleared" will be printed to the screen-tape).

Screen-tape entries can be Cut, Copied and Pasted to the Macintosh clipboard for transfer to other applications and accessories in the standard manner. To clear the screen tape, *select* the entire screen tape by clicking, holding and dragging downward until all entries appear white on black. Choose *Clear* from the **Edit** menu.

Calculator+ Keys

The calculation keys include:

- − Subtraction
- + Addition
- * Multiplication
- ÷ Division

Calculator+ offers some very useful memory keys with the following functions:

MR is *Memory Recall* and is used to bring up the value last stored to memory.

MC is *Memory Clear* and is used to clear the value stored to memory.

M+ is *Memory Plus* the value displayed in the calculator window.

M− is *Memory Minus* the value displayed in the calculator window.

Use of the memory keys is best exemplified by adding the following subsets: 2+2=4; 3+3=6; 4+4=8

2+2=4 Click **2+2=** and 4 is displayed. Now click **M+** to store the displayed subtotal in memory (actually adding 4 to 0 in memory). When a number is stored in memory, an "M" is displayed in the calculator window.

3+3=6 Click **3+3=** and 6 is displayed. Click **M+** to add 6 (displayed value) to 4 (memory value). Click **MR** to recall the new number in memory, which is now 10.

4+4=8 Click **4+4=** and 8 is displayed. Again click **M+** to add 8 to the memory value. Click **MR** to recall the new memory value of 18.

To clear memory, click the **MC** button. The "M" indicator will be removed from the calculator window.

Calculator+ offers the following algebraic functions:

√‾	Square root	Click **9** **√‾** = 3
ln	Natural Log	Click **10** **ln** = 2.302585092994
eX	e to the power of X	Click **1** **eX** **3**= 2.718281828459
xY	variable x to the power of Y	Click **2** **xY** **3**= 8
±	*sign change* of entered number	*Click* **2** ± = changes to −2
Π	pi	Click **Π** to enter 3.1415926535898
E	Exponential	Click **5 E 10** = 50000000000

*When the calculation result exceeds 10^{12} (1,000,000,000,000) or goes below 10^{-8} (0.000000001), it is automatically displayed in expotential notation.

The following trigonometric functions are provided:

sin	sine of entered value	Click **1** **sin** = .8414709848079
cos	cosine of entered value	Click **1** **cos** = .54030230586814
tan	tangent of entered number	Click **1** **tan** = 1.5574077246549
atn	arctangent of entered number	Click **1** **atn** = .78539816339745

The following financial functions are available:

Int Used to set the interest rate in financial calculations listed below. To enter a 12% interest rate, simply click: **.12 Int.** Your interest rate must match the period used for your calculations (usually yearly or monthly).

FV The Future Value Key (FV)—This calculates how much an initial investment will grow to. For example, to determine how much $500 will grow to at 15% annual interest rate in 6 years:

- **Enter *.15* and click *Int* to set the periodic interest rate.**
- **Enter *500* for the initial investment, then click *FV.***
- **Enter *6* for the number of periods, then click =.**

The initial investment will grow to $1156.53

PV The Present Value Key (PV). This calculates how much a future return is worth. For example, to determine how much $1500 will be worth in 20 years at a fixed annual interest rate of 15%:

- **Enter *.15* and press *Int* to set the periodic interest rate**
- **Enter *1500* for the final return, then click *PV.***
- **Enter *20* for the number of periods, then click =.**

The investment is worth over $91.65

Ax The Annuity key (Ax). This calculates how much a future stream level of payments is worth. For example, to determine how much $100 at the end of every year for 12 years will be worth at 15% fixed annual interest rate:

- **Enter *.15* and press *Int* to set the periodic interest rate.**
- **Enter *100* for the annuity amount, then press *Ax*.**
- **Enter *12* for the number of periods, then click = .**

The annuity is worth just over $542.06.

LP The level payment plan (LP). This calculates the level payment necessary to pay off a loan. For example, to determine how large a payment it will take to pay off a $2000 loan over three years at 18% interest, using monthly payments:

- **Enter *.015* and press *Int* for the interest rate (i.e. 18/12%, or 1.5% for a monthly interest rate).**
- **Enter *2000* for the loan amount, then click *LP*.**
- **Enter *36* for the number of periods (3 years= 36 months) then click = .**

You will see that the monthly payment is only $72.31 (rounding up to the next penny).

Most Calculator+ entries can be entered from the Macintosh keyboard:

Calculator+ Key	**Keyboard Key**
sin	s
cos	c
tan	t
atn	a
Int	Shift+I
FV	Shift+F
PV	Shift+P
Ax	Shift+A
LP	Shift+L
$\sqrt{}$	Option+V
Ln	l
eX	e
xY	x
±	Shift+Option+ =
C	Shift+C
−	−
+	*Shift*+ =
*	Shift+8
÷	/
π	Option+p
E	Shift+E
=	= or Enter

CALENDAR BOOK

The CalendarBook accessory available from the **Apple** pull-down menu and the CalendarBook available from the SideKick application operate identically. They share common data files; information recorded into one is automatically recorded into the other. The Monthly Calendar with daily notepage plus Week-at-a-Peek are included in the CalendarBook accessory. For details about operating the CalendarBook, refer to the chapter on SideKick as an application (page 66).

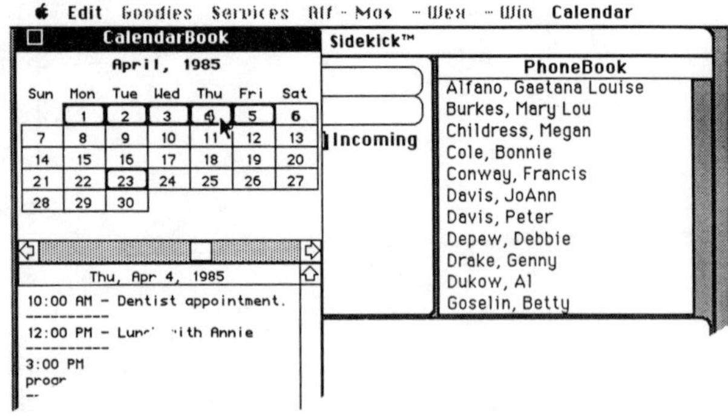

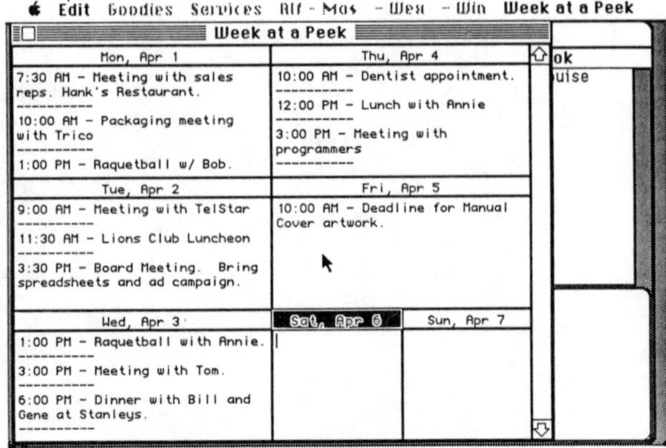

MACCLOCK

MacClock is a convenient analog clock with a sweep second hand. The time settings are regulated by the system clock, which can be adjusted with either the control panel or the system alarm clock. Like all SideKick accessories, MacClock may be positioned anywhere on the display by clicking, holding and dragging the title bar of the window.

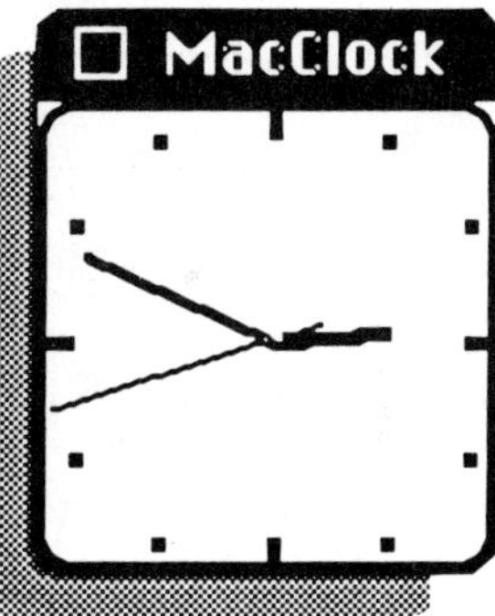

MACDIALER

The MacDialer accessory is an abbreviated version of the SideKick application program. Unlike the application, the MacDialer accessory allows you to automatically dial a phone number without having to quit the program you are working in.

The MacDialer accessory makes available all of the other telephone features found in the application: Outgoing and incoming calls can be logged with phone notes appended to the log; time stamping and billing features are recorded to the log; long distance services are available; PhoneBooks can be changed.

There are important differences between the SideKick application and the MacDialer accessory. Most notable is the inability to view the PhoneLog from the accessory. Although calls are logged from the accessory, the PhoneLog information must be viewed from the SideKick application. Sorting, printing and other PhoneLog operations are also performed trom the application program.

Another important difference between the MacDialer accessory and the SideKick application is the limited ability to enter new names into the PhoneBook from the accessory. The SideKick application places no limits on the number of entries that can be entered into the PhoneBook files.The MacDialer accessory limits you to ten entries. This number is renewed each time you run the application.

Abbreviated version of SideKick pulldown menus. Notice **Dialer** has been added to the menu bar.

Dialing status window

Active name window

Active number window

Time-stamp and billing

PhoneBook filename

PhoneBook window

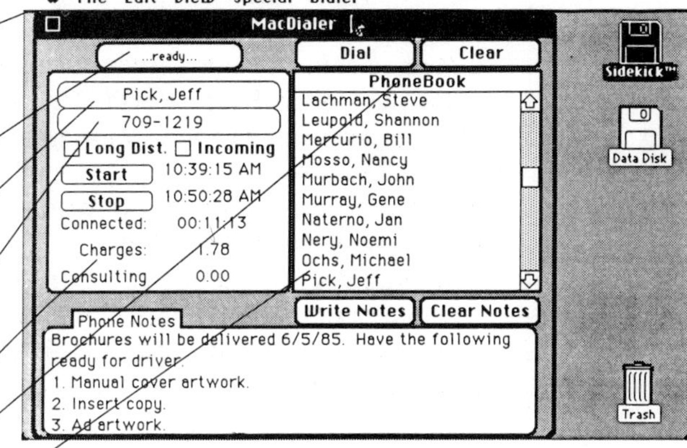

Note that the Calendar and Keypad buttons are missing from the accessory. This isn't too much of a problem since the same CalendarBook with Week-at-a-Peek is available from the **Apple** pull-down menu and can overlay MacDialer; telephone numbers can be typed manually into the active phone number window and dialed by clicking the **Dial** button.

MacDialer will access any number of PhoneBooks created from the application. Therefore, essentially all input features of the SideKick application are available in the MacDialer and Calendar accessories. The buttons and windows of the MacDialer accessory operate and function identically to those of the application program.

Dialing From The PhoneBook:

Clicking a name in the PhoneBook window automatically enters the name and phone number into the active windows. *Name*, *company*, *address*, *category* and *miscellaneous notes* of the selected number are also momentarily displayed.

If the number selected uses a long distance service (as specified on the index card), the **Long Dist.** box will have an "X" and the service selected in the **Dialer** pull-down menu will be dialed. New long distance services must be entered from the SideKick application.

Clicking the **Dial** button will initiate the call. The status window will change from "Ready" to "Pick up phone." Pick up your telephone handset and listen for dial tone. The tones will sound and the status window will read "Online."

Note: If the call is not dialed successfully, refer to ***Placing a Telephone Call*** *in SideKick application. The dial speed may have to be adjusted or pauses inserted. The rate of tone output is determined by the set dial speed option of the* ***Goodies*** *pull-down menu from the SideKick application.*

Timing The Call

Once a call is dialed, the time stamping features begin. Included are the *Start* time, the *Current* time and the time *Connected*. Phone Charges and Consulting fees are also presented. Since MacDialer cannot determine when the call actually begins (when the person called picks up the handset), you will have to click the **Start** button to accurately set the start time. Connected time and Charges will be reset.

As with the SideKick application program, clicking the **Stop** button will record the call to the PhoneLog (if Log Calls is selected) and convert the **Stop** button to **Resume**. The **Resume** button is used when you are placed on hold. Clicking the **Resume** button will resume the timing for Consulting fees, and update the time connected and phone charges while being placed on hold. Clicking the **Resume** button converts it back to the **Stop** button and initiates another start time to the PhoneLog. Clicking the **Stop** button again will log this portion of the call.

Phone Notes

The MacDialer accessory has a place for entering memos about your phone calls. The Phone Notes window is located at the bottom of the display and is always ready for keyboard entry. Notes may be entered during a phone call, and appended to the PhoneLog for that call by clicking the **Write Notes** button. The notes should then be cleared by clicking the **Clear Notes** button. As in the application program, notes can be copied, cut and pasted to other accessories from the **Edit** pull-down menu.

Incoming Calls

Incoming calls can be recorded in the PhoneLog by clicking the **Incoming** box on the MacDialer display. If the person calling is registered in the current PhoneBook, click the name in the PhoneBook window to have it automatically entered in the active windows. If the person is not registered in the PhoneBook, you must manually type in the name and phone number into these windows:

- **Click the active name window and type in the name.**
- **Press Tab or Return.**
- **Type in the phone number for future reference.**
- **Click the Start button to begin the timing of the call.**
- **Click the Stop button to end the timing of the call.**

The incoming call will be recorded in the PhoneLog without any phone charges accrued. The log entry is labeled with an [in] to identify the call as incoming. The PhoneLog can only be viewed with the SideKick application.

Note: Consulting fees will automatically be assessed for the incoming call of clients included in the current PhoneBook. Charges to those not included must be manually calculated according to the connect time recorded in the PhoneLog.

Dialer Pull-Down Menu

The MacDialer accessory has a unique pull-down menu:

- **Point, click and hold the Dialer pull-down menu.**

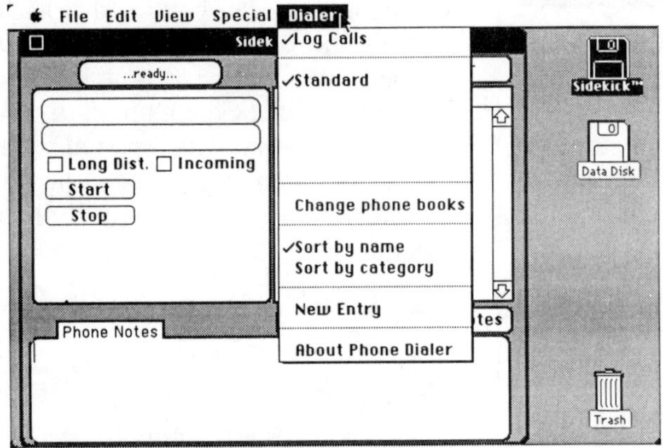

The menu commands include:

Log Calls—Used to activate (or deactivate) the recording of calls to the PhoneLog. *Choosing* this command will either place (or remove) a check next to *Log Calls*. If checked, the calls will be logged.

Standard—This space of the menu is reserved for the long-distance services for a particular PhoneBook. The service checked (by *choosing*) is the one to be used if the selected name has the *Use long-distance service* option checked on the PhoneBook index card.

Change PhoneBooks—Used to change the PhoneBook currently displayed. *Choosing* this command presents a file menu listing all of the available PhoneBook files. Buttons are present for changing drives or disks (**Eject**). The PhoneBook you want to use should be clicked to highlight the name, followed by clicking the **Open** button. The selected PhoneBook will appear in the PhoneBook window.

Sort by name—Sorts and displays the current PhoneBook alphabetically by name.

Sort by category—Sorts and displays the current PhoneBook alphabetically by category.

New Entry—Used to enter new names into the current PhoneBook. MacDialer is limited to ten entries. This number is renewed each time you use the SideKick application.

The personal index cards presented for the MacDialer accessory differ slightly from the SideKick application. The Phone costs and Consulting Fee fields are not present in the accessory. This information can be included when the index cards are viewed with the application.

About Phone Dialer—Help screen for MacDialer.

NOTEPAD +

One of SideKick's most useful accessories is Notepad+ —a mini word processor that creates Macintosh text files compatible with MacWrite™ and MicroSoft's Word.™ With Notepad+ available in the "background" of non-word processing software, such as spreadsheet, graphic and paint programs, your fleeting thoughts, important notes and even multiple page documents can be typed and saved without quitting the current application.

Besides being compatible with Macintosh's most popular word processors, Notepad+ is designed to integrate with all applicable SideKick accessories. MacTerm, for example, can read and transmit any Notepad+ file by modem. ReadiPrinter can print any Notepad+ file without tying-up your Macintosh. As in all SideKick accessories, the Notepad+ window may be displayed simultaneously with other accessories. Many of the windows, including Notepad+'s, have grow boxes to aid in positioning.

When Notepad+ is selected from the **Apple** pull-down menu, a file menu is presented.

- **Choose *Notepad+* from the Apple pull-down menu.**

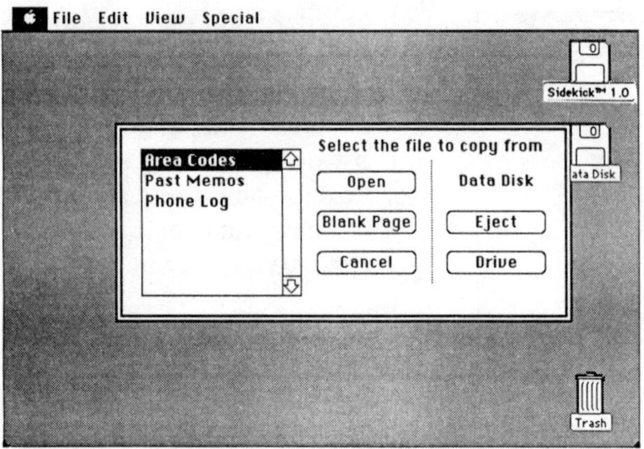

The file menu includes all of the Macintosh text files present on the disk. A Macintosh text file is any word processing document which is saved as "text only." Not included in these documents are page formats, fonts, styles, etc. The options available with the Notepad+ file menu are:

1. Select any of the listed text files by clicking the document title and the **Open** button (or by double-clicking the document title).
2. Click the **Blank Page** button to create a new Notepad+ document.
3. Click the **Drive button** to scan for text files on the disk located in another disk drive.
4. **Eject** the current disk. Inserting a new disk will present a new list of text files.
5. **Cancel** the operation.

For this discussion, select option 2:

■ **Click the Blank Page button.**

A blank page is presented.

Notepad+ uses the edit commands available in the **Edit** pull-down menu. Characters, words and lines are highlighted in the typical Macintosh manner. Highlighted text can be *Cut, Copied* and *Pasted* to and from the primary clipboard.

As in most other SideKick accessories, Notepad+ has its own unique pull-down menu.

■ **Point to the *Notepad+* pull-down menu, click and hold.**

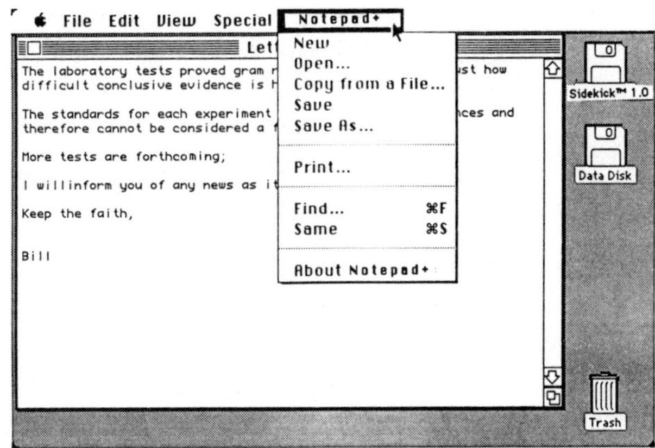

The following commands are described below:

New—Used to present a new blank page. If the current Notepad+ text has not been saved, a dialogue box will request that you do so.

Open...—Used to open a new text file. Selecting this option will present choices available from the text file menu.

Copy from a File—Used to combine text from different Notepad+ text files. Selecting this command will present the text file menu for the current disk. The title selected will merge with the current text displayed in Notepad+. The merge is positioned into the current text at the site where the cursor last resided. Extraneous text from the copied document can be deleted with the Clear edit command.

Save—Used to save the current document as a text file. Each Notepad+ file is unique and distinguished by its title. Text file icons differ slightly from document icons having less text on the sheet.

Save As...—Used to name and save the current document as a text file.

Print—Used to print the current document.

Find...—Used to search for a word string of characters. The Find command disregards word breaks or case. Words found will be highlighted.

Same—Used to continue the search for the word requested in the Find command. Selecting this command will highlight the next occurrence of the word.

About Notepad+—Help screen.

QUIKSHEETS

The next item listed in the Apple pull-down menu is *QuikSheets*. This accessory is unique in that it is actually a combination of four separate accessories, which include Alarms, Expenses, Credit Cards and Things-To-Do. All sheets can be printed in regular page format by choosing Print from the QuikSheets pull-down menu. They can also be printed using Traveling SideKick for the Macintosh.

The four sheets are arranged as a notepad with the bottom-left corner turned up, revealing the corner of the sheet below. Clicking the underlying sheet will present the next sheet. Paging through the sheets in either direction is simply a matter of clicking the bottom left corner.

To bring up the QuikSheets accessory:

■ **Choose *QuikSheets* from the Apple pull-down menu.**

The pad will be presented with multiple Alarms as the top sheet. To page through QuikSheets' collection:

■ **Click the turned-up corner to flip to the preceding sheet.**

The Things-To-Do sheet is presented.

■ **Click the turned-up corner to flip to the preceding sheet.**

The Things-To-Do sheet is presented.

■ **Click the turned-up corner to flip to the preceding sheet.**

Credit Cards is presented.

■ **Click the turned-up corner to flip to the preceding sheet.**

Expenses is presented.

■ **Click the turned-up corner to flip to the preceding sheet.**

The cycle has been completed once you've returned to Alarms. A menu common to all of the sheets is the **QuikSheets** pull-down menu. The commands listed in this menu are defined below:

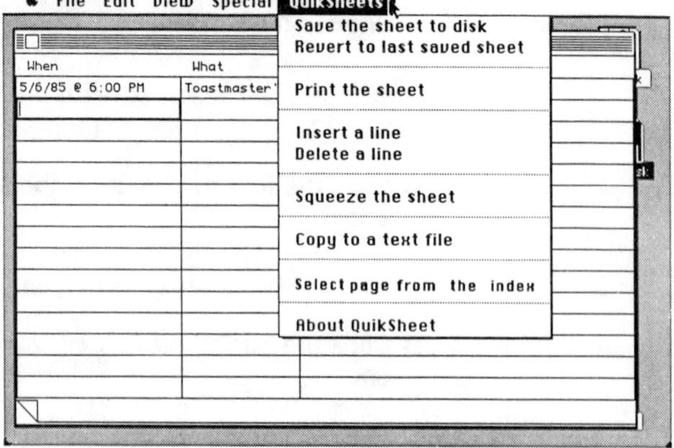

QuikSheets Menu

Save the sheet to disk—Used to save the displayed sheet to disk. *Choosing* this command will save the current sheet to the QuikSheets file on the data disk.

Revert to last saved sheet—Replaces the displayed sheet with the version last saved.

Print the sheet—Prints the displayed sheet.

Insert a line—Used to insert a line at the current location of the editing cursor. If the sheet is full, *Insert a Line* will push the bottom entry off the list.

Delete a line—Used to remove the line designated by the editing cursor.

Squeeze the sheet—Used to tighten the list. Selecting this command will remove the blank lines from the list and push entries towards the top. This command will remove the checked-off entries from Things-To-Do and past events from Alarms if displayed.

Copy to a text file—Used to save the displayed sheet to disk as a text file. This command provides a way to store the sheets as a permanent record available to other accessories and applications. Any text file can be viewed with Notepad+ and printed by ReadiPrinter.

Select a page from the index—Presents an index of sheets to choose from. This allows you to select a sheet without having to scroll through the pad.

About QuikSheets—A help screen for Quiksheets.

Entries are made into QuikSheets by clicking a field and typing the appropriate information. Pressing Tab or Return will move the cursor into the next field. Each time you change sheets or close the QuikSheets pad altogether, the displayed sheet will be saved to disk. The next time you open QuikSheets, the first sheet presented will be the sheet you previously closed from.

All sheets use the editing commands of the **Edit** pull-down menu. Since the *Cut*, *Copy* and *Paste* commands support the Macintosh clipboard, information can be easily transferred between accessories and other applications.

Although they share many similarities, each sheet has unique characteristics that should be discussed.

ALARMS

SideKick's multiple Alarms notifies you of important time events, such as appointments, reminders, etc. Alarms can hold up to 15 events. To enter an alarm:

- **Point to the first *When* field and double-click.**

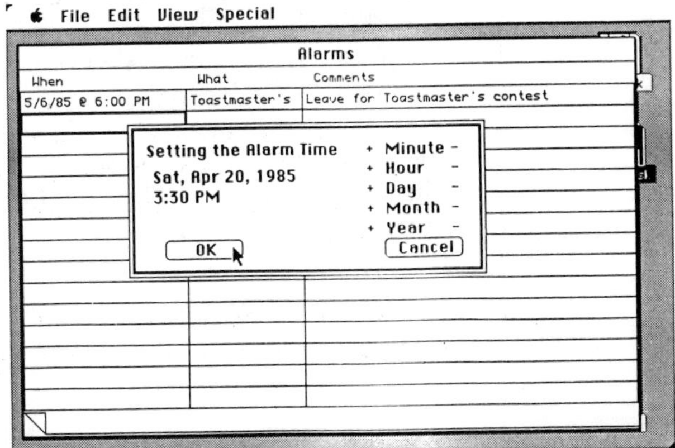

A window used to set the time and date of the entry appears. The current time and date are presented along with controls for setting the alarm. Click the + or – for each control to set the time and date of an event.

The alarm setting is automatically entered into the *When* field.

- **Press Tab or Return to highlight the *What* field.**
- **Type *What* the appointment's about (luncheon, doctor, call home, etc.). Press Tab or Return to highlight the *Comments* field.**
- **Type any *Comments* about the alarm (address, phone number, etc.).**

You can press Tab or Return for another alarm entry. Click the highlighted *When* field to present the time setting window. Repeat the procedure for entering another alarm.

Alarm Activation

When an alarm is activated, the Macintosh bell will sound and the apple of the **Apple** pull-down menu will flash. This is your signal to choose the *Quiksheets* accessory from the Apple menu and view the reminder.

A dialogue box will note the *When, What* and *Comments* of the alarm. You are also given the option of keeping the entry in the Alarms list (**Keep for Rescheduling**) or removing the entry (**Remove**). Selecting the latter option will permanently remove the alarm entry.

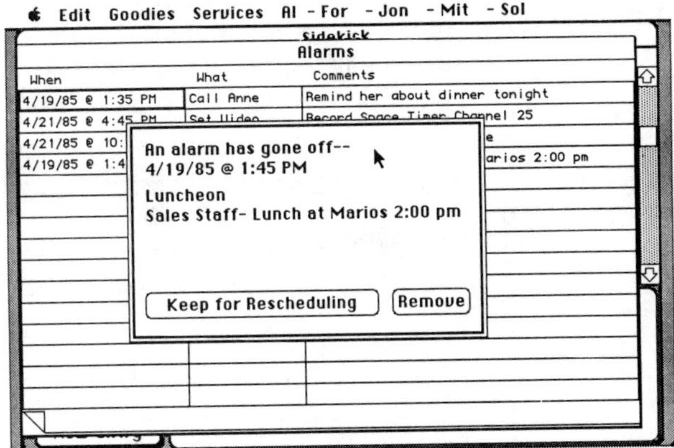

Once your list of alarms has been entered, click the turned-up corner of the Alarms sheet to present Things-To-Do. The current Alarms list will be saved to disk.

■ **Click the turned-up corner of the Alarms sheet.**

THINGS-TO-DO

SideKick's Things-To-Do sheet is a convenient place for you to list tasks that must be performed. It provides for fifteen entries, and an easy-to-use check and remove operation for updating the list.

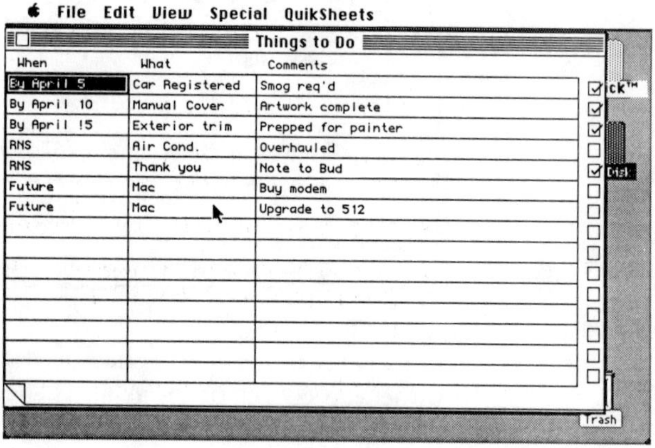

File Edit View Special QuikSheets

Things to Do

When	What	Comments	
By April 5	Car Registered	Smog req'd	☑
By April 10	Manual Cover	Artwork complete	☑
By April !5	Exterior trim	Prepped for painter	☑
RNS	Air Cond.	Overhauled	☐
RNS	Thank you	Note to Bud	☑
Future	Mac	Buy modem	☐
Future	Mac	Upgrade to 512	☐

Trash

Tasks entered into Things-To-Do are described by the three column heads: *When, What* and *Comments. When* is used to describe the time limitations for performing the task; *What* is used to describe the nature of the task; *Comments* is used for any additional information about the task. The boxes to the far right of each line are used to check-off tasks that have been performed.

Information is entered into Things-To-Do in the same manner as the *What* and *Comments* fields of the Alarms accessory. Clicking a field will outline the selection and provide an editing cursor for typing. Double-clicking will highlight a field for the **Edit** pull-down menu commands or the **QuikSheets** menu line editing commands.

To enter a task into Things-To-Do:

- **Type *When* the thing has to get done and press Tab or Return to enter the *What* field.**
- **Type *What* has to be done and press Tab or Return.**
- **Any additional information can be entered in the *Comments* field. Press Tab or Return for another TTD entry.**

A **QuikSheets** pull-down menu command that functions differently for Things-To-Do is *Squeeze the list.* For Things-To-Do this command is designed to remove tasks that have been checked off.

Each time you close the Things-To-Do display or flip to another sheet, the list will be automatically saved to disk.

- **Click the turned-up corner of the Things-To-Do sheet to flip to Credit Cards.**

CREDIT CARDS

The Credit Cards sheet is used to maintain a record of your credit card activities. The sheet provides a place to record your credit card numbers, expiration dates, lost card report information, credit lines and available balances.

The Credit Cards sheet automatically totals the credit limit and available balance for all of your credit cards. To enter your credit card information:

- **Point to the first *Company* field and click.**
- **Type in the company name and press Tab or Return.**
- **Type in the card *Number* and press Tab or Return.**
- **Type in the card expiration date and press Tab or Return.**

The *Lost Report* field is used to reference a lost credit card report. If the card being entered is not lost:

- **Press Tab or Return.**
- **Type in the line of credit extended for this card. Press Tab or Return.**
- **According to your last statement, type in the available balance for this card. Press Tab or Return.**

Repeat these steps for all other credit card entries.

Note: Credit Card & Expense entries must be entered as whole integers. Entries that are fractions of a dollar should be rounded-up or down and then entered as an integer.

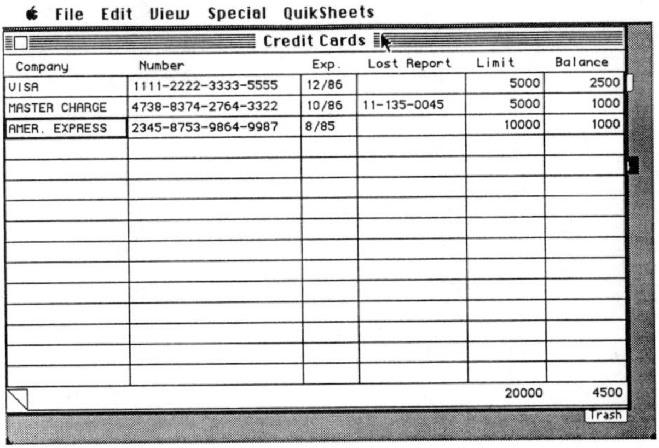

File Edit View Special QuikSheets

Credit Cards

Company	Number	Exp.	Lost Report	Limit	Balance
VISA	1111-2222-3333-5555	12/86		5000	2500
MASTER CHARGE	4738-8374-2764-3322	10/86	11-135-0045	5000	1000
AMER. EXPRESS	2345-8753-9864-9987	8/85		10000	1000
				20000	4500

Trash

Each time you close the Credit Cards display or flip to another sheet, the current information will be automatically saved to disk.

■ **Click the turned-up corner of the Credit Cards sheet to flip to Expenses.**

EXPENSES

SideKick's Expenses accessory is a convenient place for you to keep a contemporaneous record of your business and travel expenses. The accessory automatically calculates the total for the listed expenses.

Expenses entered are described by: *What, Who, When* and *Amount. What* is used to describe the type of expense (luncheon, taxi, hotel,etc.); *Who* is used to name the person, company or other reference for the expense; *When* is used to time-stamp the expense; the *Amount* field is for the actual amount of the expense.

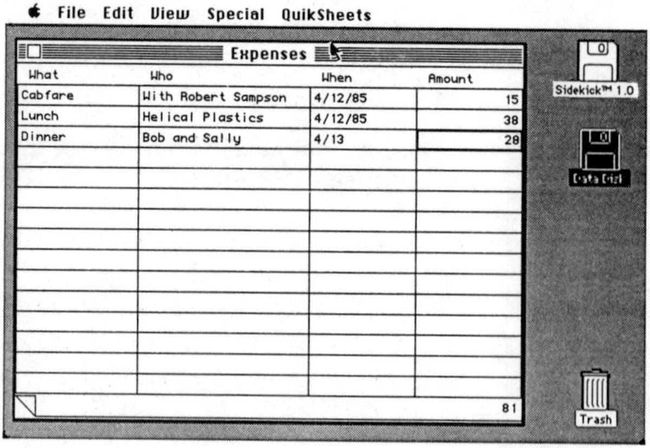

File Edit View Special QuikSheets

Expenses

What	Who	When	Amount
Cabfare	With Robert Sampson	4/12/85	15
Lunch	Helical Plastics	4/12/85	38
Dinner	Bob and Sally	4/13	28
			81

Sidekick™ 1.0

Trash

Information is entered into Expenses much like the Credit Cards. Clicking a field will outline the selection and provide an editing cursor for typing. Double-clicking will highlight a field for **Edit** pull-down menu commands or **QuikSheets** menu line editing commands.

To enter your expenses:

- **Click the *What* field of the first line.**
- **Type *What* the expense was for and Press Tab or Return to enter the *Who* field.**
- **Type in the name of the person or company *Who* received or benefited from the expense. Press Tab or Return.**
- **Type in the time and date of the expense and press Tab or Return.**
- **Enter the *Amount* of the expense (round-off to the nearest dollar). Press Tab or Return for the next entry.**

Although Expenses provides for a maximum of fifteen entries, the list may be printed and saved as a text file for a permanent record of your expenses. It is suggested that you save the files under a name that references the date for the listed expenses. It's highly recommended that you make hard copies of each expense report.

Each time you close the Expenses display or flip to another sheet, the report currently displayed will be automatically saved to disk.

- **Exit QuikSheets by clicking the close box of the Credit Cards display.**

MACTERM

MacTerm is SideKick's terminal program used to operate Hayes-compatible 300, 1200 and 2400 baud modems. Since the accessory resides in the **Apple** menu, you are able to transmit and receive data while running other applications. MacTerm's most notable features include full integration with Notepad+ text files and automatic dialing from a multiple listing directory.

MacTerm has a special configuration utility used to establish the parameters for your particular modem. This utility is available from the finder (i.e., SideKick desktop) and accessed by double-clicking the MacTerm Configuration icon.

To configure SideKick for your modem, open the SideKick disk icon to present its desktop:

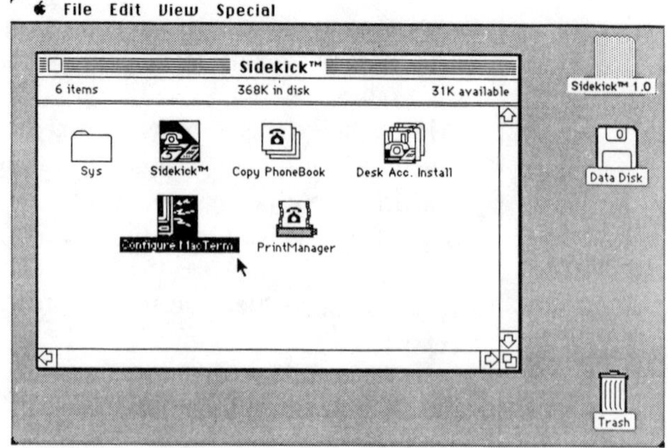

- **Double-click the SideKick disk icon.**
- **Double-click the MacTerm Configuration icon.**

The configuration window will appear with standard defaults selected. As indicated, information about the connecting port, initial baud rate, parity, stop bits, and data length are defined.

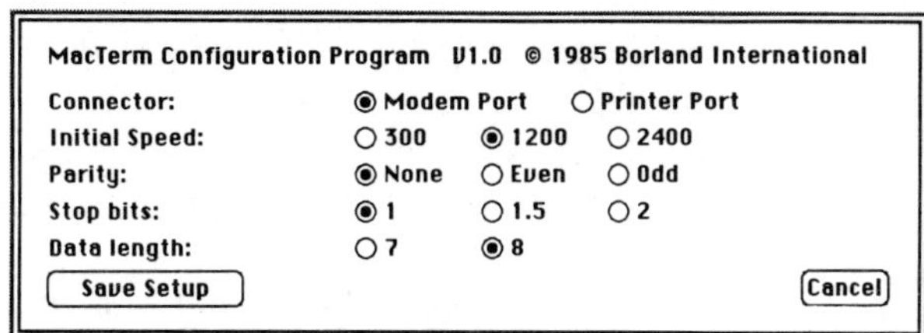

The *connecting port* option allows you to connect your modem to either the modem or printer serial ports of your Macintosh. This option is particularly convenient for users with hard disks connected to their modem serial port.

The *initial baud rate* determines the rate of communication for normal use. The rate defined in the MacTerm Configuration utility is the rate automatically selected each time you use MacTerm. There is, however, a baud rate adjustment menu available in the MacTerm accessory. This feature allows you to adjust communication speeds without having to reconfigure MacTerm.

Parity, stop bits and *data length* are controls determined either by your particular modem or your personal needs. Consult the user manual provided with your modem to establish the proper settings.

Once you have configured MacTerm:

- **Click the *Save* button.**

The configuration is saved to the SideKick master disk, filed in the MacTerm Configuration utility.

Using MacTerm

Like all SideKick accessories, MacTerm is available from the **Apple** pull-down menu.

- **Point to the Apple pull-down menu and choose *MacTerm.***

The MacTerm data window is presented. With the modem powered up, you can "talk" to your modem through standard "AT" commands. Refer to your modem manual for the command set specific to your modem. Dialog between your keyboard and modem as well as between modems is displayed in the data window. Keyboard activity is displayed only when your modem's *local echo* command is activated.

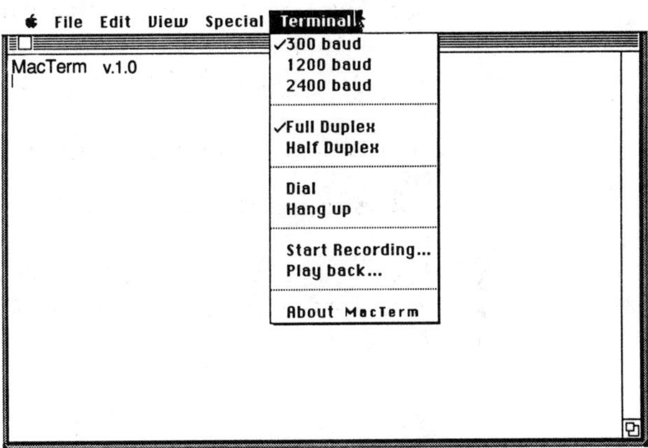

MacTerm has its own pull-down menu:

■ **Point, click and hold the *Terminal* pull-down menu.**

The available commands are:

300—Adjusts the communication rate to 300 bits per second.

1200—Adjusts the communication rate to 1200 bits per second.

2400—Adjusts the communication rate to 2400 bits per second.

Full Duplex—Used for the simultaneous transmission of data in two directions.

Half Duplex—Used for the transmission of data in one direction.

Dial—Used to display MacTerm's directory and automatically dial a selected number. The dial command converts to **Stop Dialing** until the call is successfully dialed.

Hang up—Used to disconnect your modem from the phone line.

Start recording...—Used to record data received to disk. This command presents a dialogue box used to title the received text file. Data that is received by your modem is automatically saved to disk. This command converts to **Stop Recording...** after being activated.

Playback...—Used to select saved text files for data transmission. This command presents a file menu to select from. Clicking the **Open** button will transmit the selected file to your modem.

MacTerm Directory

Numbers that you frequently dial by modem may be stored in MacTerm's directory. The numbers included in the directory are automatically dialed when selected. The directory is presented by choosing the ***Dial*** option of the **Terminal** pull-down menu.

- **Choose *Dial* from the Terminal pull-down menu.**

The directory allows for seven commonly used numbers. To make an entry:

- **Type the name of the service. Press Tab.**
- **Type the phone number of the service. Press Tab.**
- **Repeat for other numbers frequently used.**
- **Click the *Save* button to save the directory to disk.**

To automatically dial a number from the directory:

- **Click the appropriate *Dial* button.**

The number selected is dialed and the MacTerm data window presented. Like other SideKick windows, the MacTerm data window's size is adjustable and movable, should you wish to do other activities while using your modem.

Received data can be saved to disk by selecting ***Start Recording...*** from the **Terminal** pull-down menu. This command should be selected after you have dialed the number and received a carrier detect signal. A dialogue box is presented for you to name the file. The data captured is automatically saved and may be viewed and printed as a Notepad+ text file. It is also visible in the MacTerm data window.

Received data which is displayed on the data window can be edited from the commands available in the **Edit** pull-down menu. *Cut, Copy* and *Paste* utilize the Macintosh clipboard so pasting to other accessories and applications is possible.

Notepad+ text files are also used for data transmission. Following carrier detection, text files can be exported to your modem by selecting the ***Playback...*** command of the **Terminal** pull-down menu. The procedure for transmitting a text file is as follows:

- **Dial a carrier from the MacTerm directory or manually by using the appropriate AT command followed by the telephone number.**
- **"OK" displayed on MacTerm's data window signifies carrier detect.**
- **Choose *Playback...* from the Terminal pull-down menu.**

A file menu is presented.

- **Select the file you wish to transmit and click the *Open* button.**

The disk drive will whir as the data is transmitted through your modem. The data sent to your modem will be displayed only if the local echo AT command was issued (refer to your modem manual for the proper command). If data is to be received during the transmission, choose ***Start Recording...*** from the **Terminal** pull-down menu. Title the file appropriately.

After the file is successfully transmitted and any received data captured:

- **Choose *Hang up* from the terminal menu to terminate the call.**

"Chatting" during modem transmission is performed from the MacTerm data window. Received data may be saved as a text file or copied to the primary clipboard and pasted to any file.

READIPRINTER

Appropriately named, ReadiPrinter is always available as an accessory to print any text file on the fly. The accessory has a software spooling capability that allows you to print the text file without tying up your Macintosh.

To use ReadiPrinter, be sure that your printer is powered and the select button depressed.

- **Choose *ReadiPrinter* from the Apple pull-down menu.**

A text file menu is presented. You have the option of viewing the text files on the other disk (**Drive** button), or ejecting the disk (**Eject**).

- **Select the text file you wish to print by clicking the file name.**
- **Click the *Print* button.**

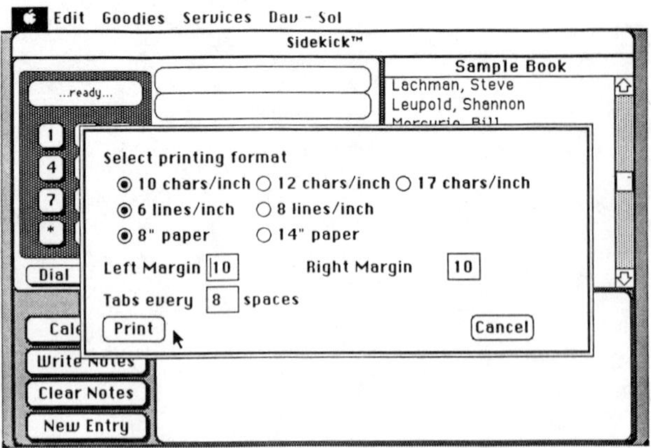

A printing format dialogue box is displayed. Since text files are saved without page layout format, this dialogue box provides the means for shaping the text. The options presented allow you to adjust the character size and line spacing of the printed document. Paper width, margin and tab settings are also available.

Since "Tab" keys are registered as a type of character, each Tab will produce the number of spaces designated in the ***Tabs every*** ☐ ***spaces*** field. This is a convenient method of indenting or producing columns in any text file.

- **Click the appropriate settings.**
- **Click the *Print* button.**

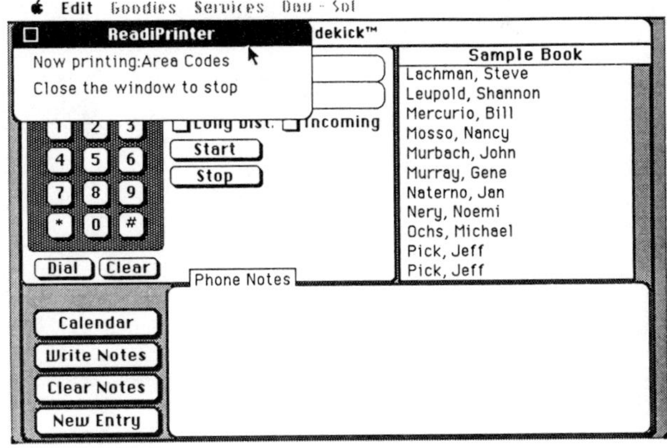

While the selected text file is being printed, notice that the keyboard and mouse are free for other activities. You may open other accessories while printing. The printing operation may be terminated at any time simply by closing the ReadiPrinter window.

To terminate the printing operation prematurely, simply click the close box of the ReadiPrinter window. The data stream to your printer will terminate, however, it may take some time for the printer buffer to empty its data.

INSTALLING SIDEKICK'S ACCESSORIES

One of SideKick's most useful features is the ability to open any of the installed accessories from the **Apple** menu while operating other Macintosh software. The only limitations placed on this background operating feature is the amount of free space available on the target disk and how closely the target software follows the Macintosh user-interface guidelines established by Apple Computer Corporation.

Neither limitation should present any serious problems. SideKick is written in the most efficient programming language possible, consuming only 32K (maximum) of target disk space with all of the accessories installed. In regards to the user-interface of the target disk: Macintosh software that doesn't follow Apple's guidelines probably isn't worth worrying about.

SideKick's accessories are transferred to other applications disks with the Desk Accessory Installer available on the SideKick master disk. This utility is also used to remove unwanted Apple or SideKick accessories. To operate the installer:

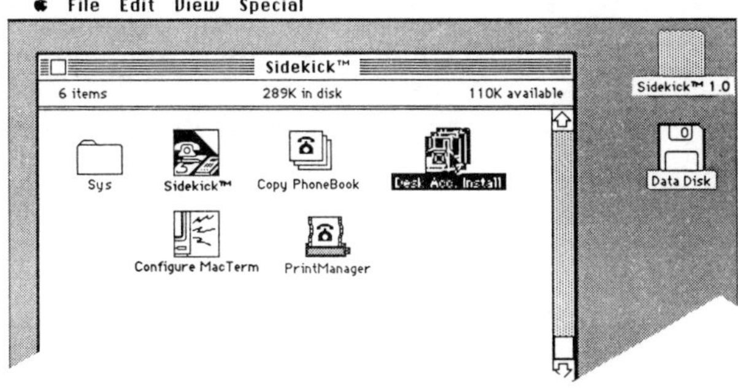

- **Double-click the *Desk Acc. Installer* icon on the SideKick desktop.**

The SideKick Accessory Installer display is presented.

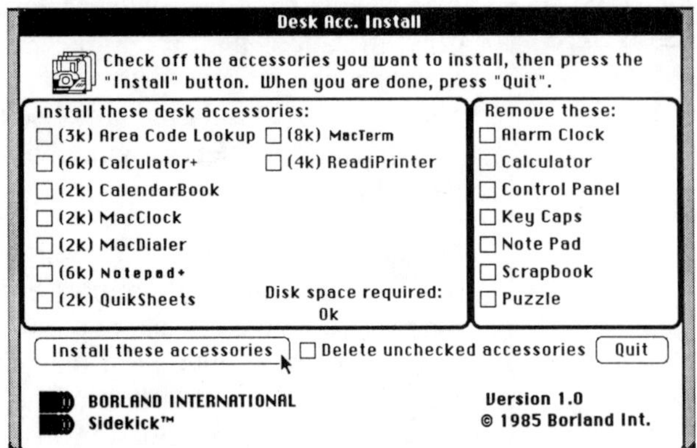

The display allows you to designate which accessories are to be installed on the target disk. The required disk space for each accessory is provided along with the cumulative disk space for the combined accessories. As you select more accessories, the disk space requirement increases.

If the option **Delete unchecked accessories** is selected, the SideKick accessories that are not checked will be removed if found on the target disk.

The Desk Accessory Installer also allows you to remove existing Apple accessories during the installation operation. Simply click to check off the unwanted accessories listed below the **Remove these:** heading.

After you've checked off the accessories you want to install and those you want to remove:

- **Click the *Install* button.**

The file menu presented lists the System folder for the SideKick master disk.

- **Click the *Drive* button.**

If the SideKick Data disk is in the external drive, the disk name will be presented. There will be no *System* folder listed in the file menu since it doesn't exist on the Data disk.

> *Note: Target disks must contain a System folder for successful installation of SideKick's accessories.*

> *Note:* ***Borland*** *is not responsible for damages to files stored on the target disk.*

- **Click the *Eject* button to remove the Data disk.**
- **Insert the target application disk to which you want the SideKick accessories installed.**

The disk title with the amount of available free space is presented. The *System* folder will also be listed in the file menu. Note that the **Install** button is now useable, and the amount of free disk space available on the target disk is presented. Also note that the amount of disk space required for installing the selected accessories is summarized at the top of the display.

- **Click the *Install* button.**

The selected accessories will be installed on the target disk. Following the installation, the file menu is again presented. You may install the same group of accessories on another target disk by clicking the **Eject** button followed by the **Install** button, or end the operation by clicking the **Cancel** button. The Cancel button will return you to the Desk Accessory Installer's main display where you may select different accessories for additional installations, or **Quit** the utility altogether.

MULTIPLE PHONEBOOKS

SideKick is designed to utilize an unlimited number of PhoneBooks, each having an unlimited number of entries. The PhoneBooks can be selected by double-clicking the appropriate PhoneBook icon on the finder or by choosing the *Change PhoneBooks* option of the pull-down menus of the SideKick application or the MacDialer accessory.

You can use one of two methods for creating new PhoneBooks. The first method should be used when you want to create a completely unique PhoneBook that has few entries common to other PhoneBooks. Follow this procedure:

- **Open the DataPhiles folder and rename the PhoneBook file something other than "PhoneBook".**
- **Close the folder and the Data disk desktop.**
- **Open the SideKick desktop and double-click the SideKick application icon.**

When the SideKick application is opened, the program searches both the master and data disks for a file named "PhoneBook". If the file cannot be found, the program creates one. The new PhoneBook file is presented in the SideKick application where you can begin making new entries.

Copy PhoneBook

The other method for creating new PhoneBooks utilizes a copy utility provided on SideKick's desktop. The utility makes a copy of those entries in the "PhoneBook" file which have the **Include in PhoneBooks** option checked on their personal index cards. To use this method:

- **Double-click the Copy PhoneBook icon on the finder.**

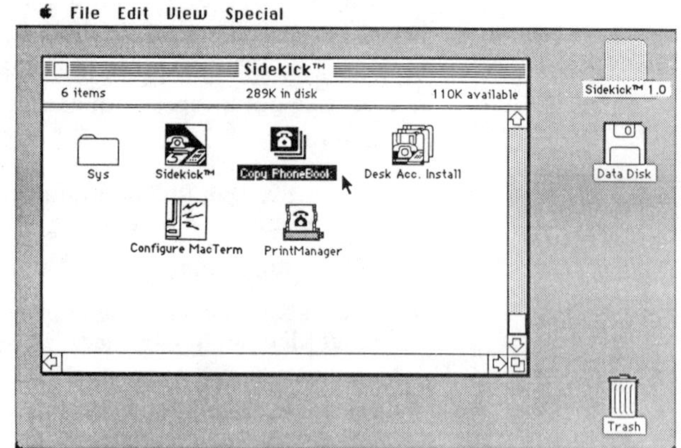

The program will search for the "PhoneBook" filename and inform you of the number of entries that are selected for inclusion in other PhoneBooks and the amount of disk space required to store the new book. Also, the option of abbreviating the entries in the new PhoneBook is offered to conserve disk space. The abbreviated entries include only the *name, telephone number* and *category* fields.

- **Click the *Copy the PhoneBook* button.**

A status box will indicate that the PhoneBook entries are being read and stored in memory.

A save dialogue box is presented for you to name the new PhoneBook and the drive you want it written to. If you want the copy saved to the same data disk, click the **Drive** button. If you want to save the new book to another disk, do so from the external disk drive: Click the **Eject** button and insert the other disk.

■ **Type in a unique filename and click the *Save* button.**

The PhoneBook will be copied to the disk designated in the save dialogue box. Afterwards, the save dialogue box is presented again for additional copies. If you have made all of the copies needed:

■ **Click the *Cancel* button to return to the "Copy Phonebook" summary display.**

■ **Click the *Quit* button.**

You will return to the finder.

PRINTMANAGER

SideKick features a powerful printing application that extracts specified information from your PhoneBook, Calendar and QuikSheets files, and prints the data in a variety of useful formats. The application is called PrintManager and is available on the SideKick desktop.

It is best to operate PrintManager with the SideKick master disk placed in the internal drive and your data disk, containing the DataPhiles folder, in the external drive. Of course, if you plan to print your Week-at-a-Peek or PhoneBook files, they must already contain information entered from either the SideKick application or the MacDialer and CalendarBook accessories. QuikSheets can be printed as blank sheets or as completed sheets containing data.

Three main displays are available in PrintManager: One for printing PhoneBook files, another for Week-at-a-Peek and a third for printing QuikSheets. The display that you *Quit* PrintManager from will be the display presented the next time you double-click the PrintManager icon. To open PrintManager:

- **Double-click the PrintManager icon on the finder.**

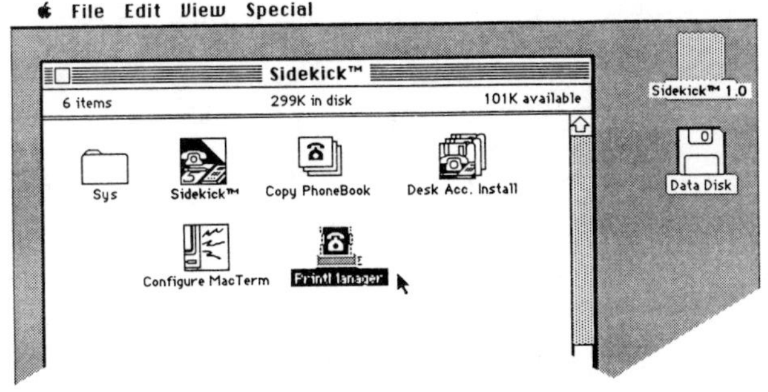

A screen is presented with three pull-down menus. It is the **Print** menu that offers the utility of PrintManager.

■ **Point to the *Print* pull-down menu, click and hold.**

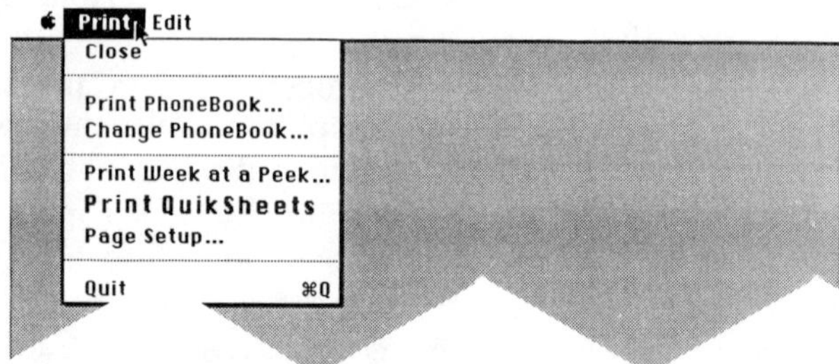

The commands available from the **Print** pull-down menu include:

Close—Used to close either the PhoneBook or Week-at-a-Peek printing displays. Clicking the close box of these displays effects the same results as the *Close* command: You return to this opening display.

Print PhoneBook...—Presents the PhoneBook printing utility.

Change PhoneBook...—Used to select among your PhoneBook files for printing.

Print Week-at-a-Peek...—Presents the Week-at-a-Peek and yearly calendar printing utility.

Print QuikSheets...—Presents the QuikSheets printing utility.

Page Set-up—Used to configure the type of paper, orientation, pagination and reduction for the print-out.

Quit—Used to exit the PrintManager application.

Print PhoneBook

The PhoneBook PrintManager allows you to sort and print your PhoneBook entries in a variety of different formats. The files may be printed or saved to disk as reports, index cards, and mailing labels. You can even merge your PhoneBook files into word processing documents created with MicroSoft's Word™ for personalized form letters.

To present the PhoneBook PrintManager display:

- **Choose *Print PhoneBook...* from the Print pull-down menu.**

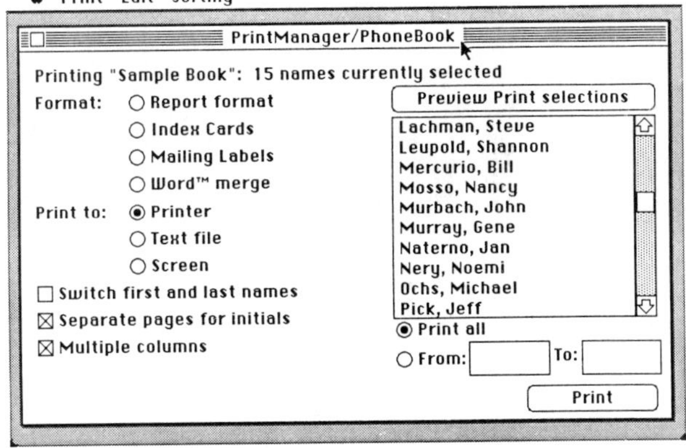

The PhoneBook PrintManager features a scrollable window that allows you to view PhoneBook entries according to the sort command selected in the **Sorting** pull-down menu. Range fields are available to limit your print-outs; a **Preview Print Selections** button allows you to view the selected range. A **Screen** button is also provided for you to evaluate the print-out on screen before printing to paper.

All of your PhoneBook files are accessible from PrintManager.

- **Choose *Change PhoneBook...* from the Print pull-down menu.**

A PhoneBook file menu is presented.

- **Click to highlight the PhoneBook file you wish to print.**
- **Click the *Open* button.**

The selected PhoneBook will be displayed in the PhoneBook window with its filename identified at the top of the display.

Sorting the PhoneBook

The current PhoneBook may be sorted by the fields listed in the **Sorting** pull-down menu.

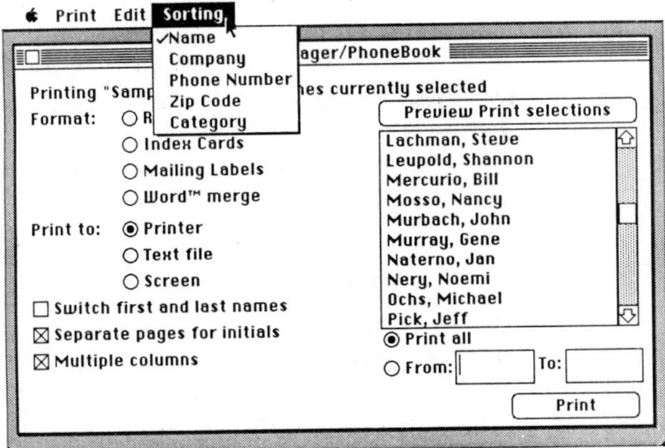

The PhoneBook window will display the entries alphabetically according to the field selected in the **Sorting** pull-down menu.

PrintManager's print range and sorting features provide you with a very flexible printing utility. For instance, you can sort the PhoneBook by *Company* and limit your print-out to a specific company by entering the appropriate alphabetic range. Or sort the PhoneBook by *Zip Code* and limit your print-out of mailing labels to a geographical region by entering the appropriate zip code range.

Note: The ***To:*** *field is not inclusive. Selecting a range of A to C will print only those sorted fields beginning with A and B. The C's will not be included.*

If you redefine the print range, entries included in the new range can be viewed in the PhoneBook window by clicking the **Preview Print Selections** button. The total number of names included in the specified range is displayed at the top of the screen.

Printing Formats

PrintManager offers a wide variety of printing formats for your PhoneBook files. The list will be printed according to the format selected, in the order designated by the sort and limited to any specified range.

You may view a sample "print-out" for each format on your Macintosh screen (to conserve on paper) by clicking the **Print to: Screen** button followed by the **Print** button. Your PhoneBook, with the selected format, will appear on the screen. A **Wait** button is available to pause the scrolling list; a **Cancel** button is present to quit the printing operation.

Before printing an actual hard copy, refer to the section on *Page Setup*. To select a format, click the appropriate **Format** button.

Report Format—Prints all of the information contained in the personal index card for each PhoneBook entry.

```
Mathis, Kerry [Data Day]______________________________________(818) 509-0474
  7650 Haskell Av_____________________________________________Van Nuys, CA 91406
  Forms          ☒ Include in menu☐ Include in books☐ Use Long Dist. Service
  Phone:1.50/min. for 3 minutes then 1.80/min.  Consult:0.00/hr.
  MacDesk binder and forms supplier.
McAffe, Illia [Redgate]_______________________________________(818) 845-8876
  2398 Park Encino Ln_________________________________________Encino, CA 91316
  Friend         ☒ Include in menu☐ Include in books☐ Use Long Dist. Service
  Phone:1.50/min. for 3 minutes then 1.60/min.  Consult:0.00/hr.
McClery, Taylor [Interconnect]________________________________(408) 973-0986
  2267 Barcroft Rd____________________________________________Cupertino, CA 95014
  Supplier       ☒ Include in menu☐ Include in books☐ Use Long Dist. Service
  Phone:0.30/min. for 3 minutes then 0.35/min.  Consult:0.00/hr.
  Phone connectors
Mercer,  Ron [Mercer Printing]________________________________(408) 973-3322
  296 Martin Dr_______________________________________________Cupertino, CA 95014
  Printer        ☒ Include in menu☐ Include in books☐ Use Long Dist. Service
  Phone:0.30/min. for 3 minutes then 0.40/min.  Consult:0.00/hr.
  Offset printing
Merch, Bob [Ralphs]___________________________________________(408) 973-5823
  667 Hether Rd_______________________________________________Los Gatos, CA 95012
  Friend         ☒ Include in menu☐ Include in books☐ Use Long Dist. Service
  Phone:0.30/min. for 3 minutes then 0.40/min.  Consult:0.00/hr.
```

Index Cards—Prints all of the personal information for each PhoneBook entry. The index cards may be printed "two-up" by selecting the **Multiple columns** option.

```
Marvin, James              Mathis, Kerry
Dalla Lease                Data Day
2341 Bedford Dr            7650 Haskell Av
Dallas, TX  72519          Van Nuys, CA  91406

(214) 521-3342             (818) 509-0474

  Auto                       Forms
```

Note: Because of CRT width limitations, the print-to-screen command cannot display multiple columns, however, the actual hard copy will be printed two-up.

Mailing Labels—Prints the *Name, Company, Address, City, State* and *Zip Code* as one-up mailing labels. The labels may be printed with first name "first" by selecting the **Switch first and last names** option.

```
Vinnie Mathews             Bob Merch
Altruistic Inc             Ralphs
5432 Henson Way            667 Hether Rd
Vermouth, Mn  34987        Los Gatos, CA  95012

Kerry Mathis               William C. Mercurio
Data Day                   Cord Electronics
7650 Haskell Av            2965 Marion Dr
Van Nuys, CA  91406        Cupertino, CA  95014
```

Word™ merge—Prints the PhoneBook file as a text file formatted for merging with Microsoft's Word word processor. This command saves the PhoneBook in merge format as a text file, so it may be read and merged with Word. To save this format as a text file, select **Word merge** and the **Print to: Text file** options. Click the **Print** button. The PhoneBook will be saved as a text file under the PhoneBook filename.

Note: Refer to the MicroSoft User Manual for merging formatted text files into Word documents.

Page Setup

Before printing a hard copy, you're encouraged to print-to-screen so you may verify the format, sort and range without wasting paper. To print to screen, simply click the **Print to: Screen** command. Once you've verified the print-out:

- **Click the *Print to: Printer* option.**

Next you must specify the *type* of paper you're printing on and *how* you want it printed:

- **Choose *Page setup* from the Print pull-down menu.**

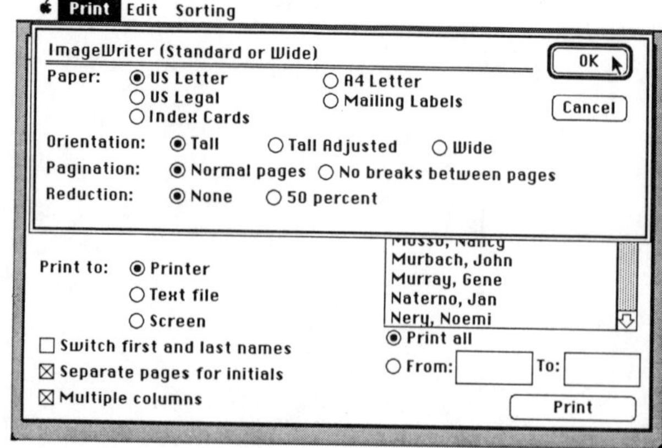

Paper—Used to select the type of paper you're printing on. Sizes include:

U.S. letter: 8½″ × 11″
U.S. legal: 8½″ × 14″
Index Cards: 4″ × 2¼″ (5 rows per sheet)
A4 letter: 8¼″ × 11⅔″
Mailing Labels: 4″ × 12″ (sheet size, 12 labels per sheet)

Orientation—Designates the orientation of the print-out. Selecting *Tall* will print the list horizontally in the standard manner. *Tall Adjusted* prints horizontally with a "heavier" and wider typeface. *Wide* prints the list sideways.

Pagination—Designates the printout to include (or not include) page breaks. If *Normal pages* is selected, each page will include top and bottom margins.

Reduction—Allows you to reduce the printout by 50%.

After establishing your page setup, it is time to print:

- **Click the *OK* button.**

You will return to the PhoneBook PrintManager display.

Print Hard Copies

To print a hard copy of the selected format, check to make sure that the **Print to: Printer** option is selected and:

■ **Click the *Print* button.**

The standard print dialogue box is presented for you to designate the *Page Range*, number of *Copies* to be printed and the type of *Paper Feed*. Enter any changes and check to make certain that your printer is connected, turned on and selected.

> *Note: Like most Macintosh printing applications, PrintManager saves a copy of the specified PhoneBook or Week-at-a-Peek range to the master disk before printing a hard copy. For extremely large files, you may have to copy certain files to another disk and delete the copied files from the master disk. A good candidate for deletion is the SideKick start-up screen; the filename is Startup Screen and is found inside the System folder on the SideKick master. The Startup Screen file is worth 22K of disk space.*

■ **Click the *OK* button.**

A dialogue box will be presented as the hard copy is printed. The printing operation may be paused by clicking the **Wait** button or cancelled by clicking the **Cancel** button.

Print Week-at-a-Peek

PrintManager offers the convenience of printing Week-at-a-Peek in a variety of formats. The ability to print any calendar week is found only in PrintManager.

To print Week-at-a-Peek with PrintManager:

- **Choose *Print Week-at-a-Peek* from the Print pull-down menu.**

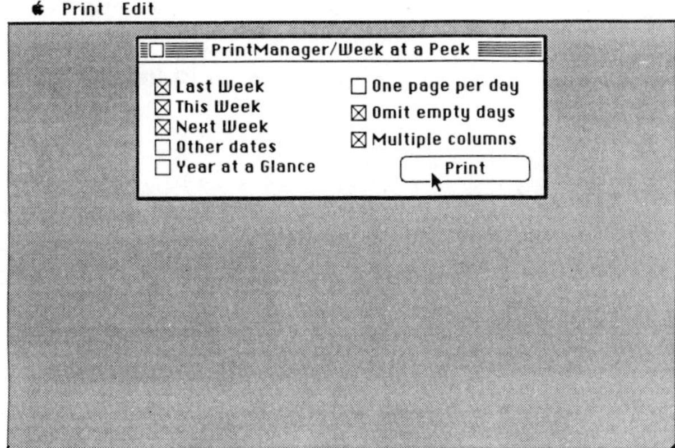

The Week-at-a-Peek print display offers you a choice of weeks to print. Simply click the box identifying **Last Week, This Week** or **Next Week** to check (or uncheck) the week you wish to print. You may select any combination for each print-out.

If you want to print other weeks, select **Other Dates**. Clicking this option will introduce two scroll bars used to specify the time range for your Week-at-a-Peek printout. Set the **Starting** and **Ending Dates** by:

- **Clicking, holding and dragging the elevator for coarse date adjustment.**
- **Clicking the elevator *shaft* to change the month.**
- **Clicking the elevator *arrows* to change the day.**
- **Clicking the *Jump to current week* button will return the time range to the current week.**

Year at a Glance

The **Year-at-a-Glance** option provides you with a printout of the yearly calendar for the current year. To print this year's calendar:

- **Click *Year-at-a-Glance.***
- **Click the *Print* button.**

You can print the calendars for a range of years by following this simple procedure:

- **Click *Year-at-a-Glance*.**
- **Click *Other dates* to introduce the range of yearly calendars you wish to print.**
- **Adjust the *Starting* and *Ending Dates* appropriately.**
- **Click the *Other dates* option to deselect the option of printing Week-at-a-Peek for the specified time range (assuming you wish only to print the yearly calendars).**
- **Click *Multiple Columns*.**
- **Click the *Print* button.**

The other options listed in the Week-at-a-Peek display include:

One page per day—If checked, the print-out will be paginated by day. If unchecked, each page will include the maximum number of *whole* days. Print-Manager will not split a day unless the daily schedule cannot fit on a single page.

Omit empty days—If checked, the print-out will include only those days with information entered. If unchecked, all days will be printed.

Multiple columns—If checked, Week-at-a-Peek will be printed two-up. If unchecked, your appointments will be printed one-up.

Page Setup

Before printing a hard copy, you must specify certain characteristics about the page layout. This is performed with the same dialogue box used with printing your PhoneBook.

■ **Choose *Page Setup...* from the Print pull-down menu.**

Specify the type of paper, the orientation, pagination and any reduction. After selecting your page setup, click the **OK** button.

Print Hard Copies

After selecting the week(s) and specifying the page setup, you're ready to print a hard copy:

■ **Click the *Print* button.**

You will be presented with the standard print dialogue box used to select the print quality, the page range, the number of copies and the type of paper feed. Enter your selections, change paper if necessary and make certain that your printer is *On* and *Selected*.

■ **Click the *OK* button.**

The printing operation will begin with the usual **Wait/Cancel** dialogue box presented to interrupt the print-out if necessary.

Print QuikSheets

The print-outs may include the entered data, or they may be printed as blank sheets for manual entry.

To print the QuikSheets:

- **Choose Print QuikSheets from the print pull-down menu.**

The Print QuikSheets display offers the following options:

- ☐ ***Multi-Columns*****—If checked, the sheets will be printed three up. Unchecked is one-up.**
- ☐ ***Leave forms blank*****—If checked, the sheets will be printed without entered data.**
- ☐ ***Select sheet individually*****—If checked, presents an index of sheets to print. If unchecked, all sheets will be printed.**

QuikSheets uses the same page setup as Week-at-a-Peek.

APPENDIX A

Installing SideKick Applications Onto Hard Disks

Follow the simple procedure outlined below for proper installation of SideKick's applications:

1. Select or create a volume on your hard disk. The selected volume must have a system folder generated from the hard disk software.

2. Insert the SideKick master disk into either disk drive and double-click the disk icon to present the desktop.

3. Click, hold and drag the **SideKick application** icon to the selected volume. Repeat for the **Desk Acc. Install, PrintManager, Copy PhoneBook** and **Configure MacTerm** icons.

4. The **DataPhiles** folder (including **Deskstuff**) must also be copied to this volume. If it is located on the SideKick master disk, click, hold and drag Data-Philes to the selected volume. If it is on a Data disk, insert the disk and follow the copy procedure.

5. Eject the SideKick master and/or Data disk.

6. To verify that SideKick has been successfully installed, run SideKick from the hard disk.

Installing SideKick Accessories Onto Hard Disks

Follow the procedures outlined below to install SideKick's desk accessories:

1. Start your hard drive.

2. To make the SideKick master disk the startup disk, insert the SideKick disk into a disk drive and open the SideKick disk. Double-click on the icon on the SideKick disk (upper right-hand side of the Mac screen) and open the *System* folder. Double-click on the icon of the *System* folder. There should now be a file with a system icon called Finder. Press the Option key and the Command key and simultaneously double-click on the system file Finder. Momentarily, the desktop will reappear with the icon of the SideKick disk in the right-hand side of the screen. The icon of the SideKick disk must be on top! (Note: For those with MacBottom hard drives, make certain that the Finder is unlocked when you install the desk accessories; otherwise, the SideKick disk icon will not be the icon to appear at the top of your screen. You can restore Finder to the locked position after you've completed installation.)

3. Now double-click on the program **Desk Acc. Install**.

4. You can now select which desk accessories to install and which to remove.

5. Click on *Install These Accessories.*

6. Click on the **Drive** button until the name over the **Eject** button is the Startup Volume of the hard drive.

7. Click on **Install**. There should be a system file on the Startup Volume.

8. Momentarily, the same menu will appear (the one with the **Install** button). Now that you're finished, you may click on **Cancel** and then on **Quit**.

APPENDIX B
CONVERTER AND QUIKEDITOR

This appendix describes the SideKick Converter and QuikEditor utilities. These tools are designed to enhance some of the other SideKick features. The SideKick Converter allows you to automatically copy phonebook entries from HabaDex, MacPhone, and various text files into your phonebook. It also automatically rearranges the fields in those files so your information can be moved into the phonebook format. QuikEditor lets you set up your own QuikSheets. You can, for example, create specialized lists of people to call, equipment you own, or any other data you can think of.

SIDEKICK CONVERTER

Warning: Before you use the Converter program, make a copy of your phonebook! You could inadvertently insert hundreds of spurious entries or do other damage to your phonebook with this program. A backup copy allows you to easily undo any mistakes you make.

SETTING UP YOUR DISKETTES

To run the Converter program, you'll need the following files on disk in your Macintosh:

- o A System Folder
- o The SideKick Converter program
- o The file you're going to convert from. This file can be the "Haba.Files" file created from HabaDex, the "PhoneBook" file from the MacPhone software (you can rename the file if you wish), or text files. We'll explain how to handle each type of file later in this appendix.

o The SideKick "PhoneBook" file to which new entries will be added. This phonebook must be named "PhoneBook" (no space between the "e" and the "B"), and is the phonebook used whenever you open SideKick or MacDialer. If the Converter program can't find a phonebook file when it starts, it will create one. Be sure that you have only one file called "PhoneBook."

If you have two disk drives, copy the Converter program onto either your SideKick main disk or the disk with the file you're converting from. Be sure there is enough free space on the phonebook disk for the new entries; you'll need about 1K for every two names you add.

If you only have one drive, you'll probably have to set up a temporary disk with the files listed above. When the Converter program is finished, don't forget to copy your phonebook back onto your SideKick disk.

STARTING THE CONVERTER

Open the program by selecting its icon and then choosing Open from the File menu, or by double-clicking the icon.

In a moment, you should see a screen that looks something like this:

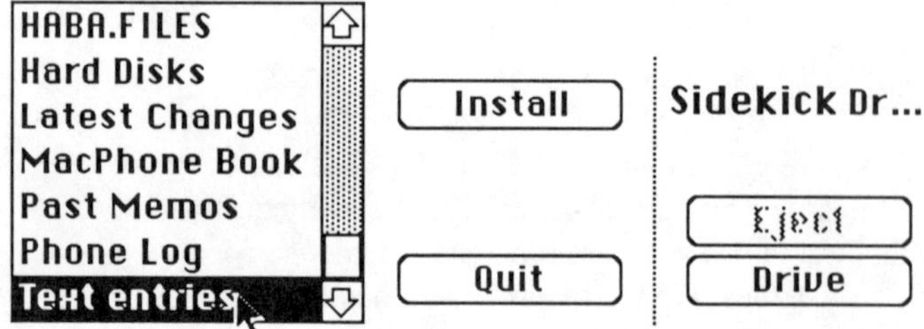

Use the Drive button to see the files on a disk in the second drive, or use the Eject button to eject the current disk so you can insert another.

Click on the name of the file you want to copy from, then click Open.

What the Convert program does now depends on the type of file being converted. Each file type is described in the following sections.

MACPHONE PHONEBOOK

If the file was created by the MacPhone software, SideKick will copy the name, phone number, first two check boxes, and billing/consultation rates into the new entries. For example, the following entry:

Name: Doe, John
Area Code: 818 Phone No: 555-1781
☒ Show in Menu Bar ☒ Use Prefix
☐ Show as a Prefix
Billing Rate: 3.00 per minute till 2 minute,
then 1.50 per minute.
☐ Show phone charges

Consultation Rate: 25.00 per hour.
◉ Show connect time
○ Show consultation charges

would be entered into the SideKick PhoneBook as:

Name: Doe, John
Company:
Address:
City: State: Zip:
Phone • Area code: 818 Number: 555-1781
Miscellaneous Notes • Category:

☒ Include in menu
☒ Include in phone books
☒ Use Long Dist. Service
☐ Round consulting fees

Phone charges •
3.00 / minute for 2 minutes then
1.50 / minute
Consulting charges • 25.00 / hour

HABADEX HABAFILES

If the file's name is "Haba.Files," the Converter program assumes that the file was created by HabaDex, and converts accordingly. For example, an entry that appears as:

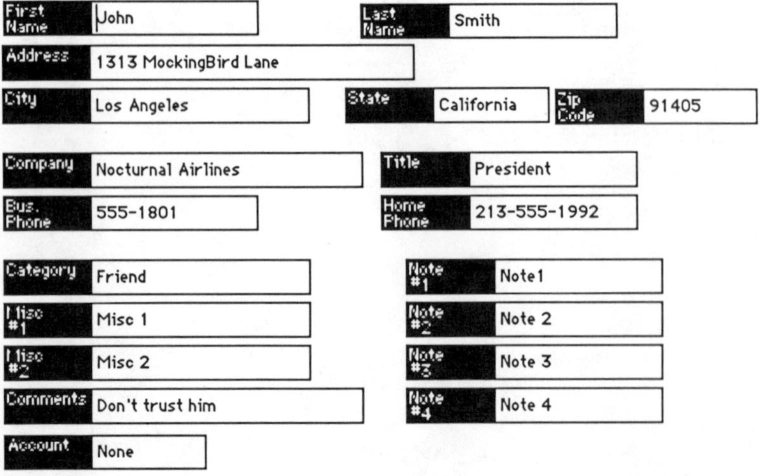
First Name: John
Last Name: Smith
Address: 1313 MockingBird Lane
City: Los Angeles
State: California
Zip Code: 91405
Company: Nocturnal Airlines
Title: President
Bus. Phone: 555-1801
Home Phone: 213-555-1992
Category: Friend
Note #1: Note1
Misc #1: Misc 1
Note #2: Note 2
Misc #2: Misc 2
Note #3: Note 3
Comments: Don't trust him
Note #4: Note 4
Account: None

would be entered into the SideKick PhoneBook as:

Name Smith, John
Company Nocturnal Airlines
Address 1313 MockingBird Lane
City Los Angeles State Calif Zip 91405
Phone • Area code Number 555-1801
Miscellaneous Notes • Category Friend

Don't trust him;None;Misc 1;Misc 2;Note1;Note 2;Note 3;Note 4;President; h. 213-555-1992

☒ Include in menu
☒ Include in phone books
☐ Use Long Dist. Service
☐ Round consulting fees

Phone charges •
0.00 / minute for 0 minutes then
0.00 / minute
Consulting charges • 0.00 / hour

The comment, note, position, home phone number, and miscellaneous entries have been combined into the miscellaneous notes section. Also, the business phone is used for the person's phone number. If no business phone is given, but a home phone is, the home number would be used instead.

The SideKick Converter program can take information from any text file and convert it into phonebook entries. Unfortunately, since there is no standard method for storing the names in the book, you'll have to tell SideKick how to interpret the file, as follows:

When you select a text file, you'll be presented with the following screen:

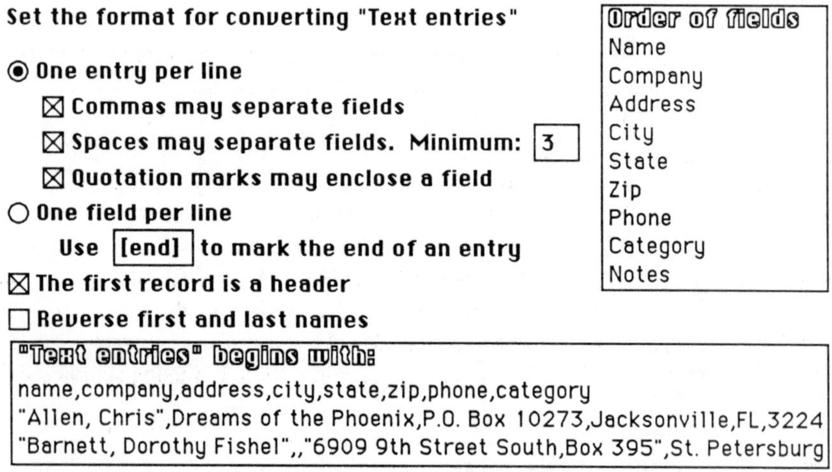

Set the format for converting "Text entries"

◉ **One entry per line**

☒ **Commas may separate fields**

☒ **Spaces may separate fields. Minimum:** 3

☒ **Quotation marks may enclose a field**

○ **One field per line**

Use [end] **to mark the end of an entry**

☒ **The first record is a header**

☐ **Reverse first and last names**

Order of fields
Name
Company
Address
City
State
Zip
Phone
Category
Notes

"Text entries" begins with:

```
name,company,address,city,state,zip,phone,category
"Allen, Chris",Dreams of the Phoenix,P.O. Box 10273,Jacksonville,FL,3224
"Barnett, Dorothy Fishel",,"6909 9th Street South,Box 395",St. Petersburg
```

The box at the bottom gives you an abbreviated look at the beginning of your file. The check boxes and circles allow you to tell the program about the text file.

When telling SideKick about the format of a text file, you must first decide whether there is "One entry per line" or "One field per line." For each person, the name, company, street address, city, state, and zip code (and probably phone number and category as well, though they aren't visible) are all on the same line. This means that you should click on the "One entry per line" box. If each piece of information were on a different line (the company on the line following the name, the address on the line following the company, and so forth), you would click on the "One field per line."

Assuming you have a file with "one entry per line," SideKick needs to know how to separate the fields--i.e., how to tell where the name ends and the company begins, for example. Many programs that create text files use a special non-printing character known as a "Tab" to separate fields. SideKick always separates two fields with a tab between them. However, not all programs use the tab for this function. Notepad+, for example, cannot have a tab in its text files.

SideKick has two other ways to separate fields: with commas or with a group of consecutive spaces. If you don't want SideKick to use either of these, click on the check boxes to uncheck them.

There is a potential problem with either of the last two separating methods: what if you want to use commas or groups of spaces as part of your information? If you allow it to, SideKick will consider anything between double quotation marks as one item, regardless of any separators in the material inside the quote marks. This allows "Adams, Chris" to be treated as a name, instead of a name of "Adams" and a company of "Chris." If you don't want this feature, click on the appropriate check box to uncheck it.

If you are working with a file that has "one field per line," there must be a special set of characters to tell SideKick where each entry ends, so it will know where the entry for "Chris Adams" ends and the entry for "Dorothy Blair" begins. If the separator is something other than "[end]," replace it with the required separator using standard editing techniques.

Regardless of whether your file has "one entry per line" or "one field per line," the first entry may not actually have any information in it. In our example, the first line is a "header" that MicroSoft Word uses for printing personalized letters. We don't want that entry included in our file, so "The first record is a header" box is checked off so that that entry will be ignored. If the first line were a name you wanted in your phonebook, you would uncheck the box.

SideKick was written with the assumption that you would format names in your phonebook with the last name first, followed by a comma, and then the first name--for example, "Blake, Donald." However, your text file may have the first name followed by the last name--"Donald Blake." If this is the case, you should check the "Reverse first and last names" box.

You're almost finished telling SideKick how to read your text file. The last piece of information you must supply is the order of the fields within an entry. SideKick assumes that each entry will have the name first, followed by the company, then the street address, city, state, zip code, phone number, category, and notes. The file can leave off the fields at the end (for example, each entry could stop at the phone number, leaving the category and notes blank), but the fields that are there must be in the order expected by SideKick.

Unfortunately, your file may not match this order. For example, let's assume your file has the company name first, then the person's name, followed by the street address, city, state, zip, and phone. To tell SideKick about the new order, simply press and hold the mouse button down over the word "Company" in the box labeled "Order of fields." It should appear in boldface (**Company**). Then, while still holding the mouse button down, drag the word up to the top. Note that "Name" automatically slides down to make room for "Company." Release the mouse button. That's it! You can rearrange any of the fields as needed to match your file.

When you have everything set just as you want it, click the OK button. SideKick will then read your entrie text file, ocnvert it as you have directed and add the new names to your phonebook.

QUIKEDITOR

QuikSheets let you keep track of several important classes of information. QuikEditor makes QuikSheets even more useful, since it allows you to create your own sheets, or tailor existing sheets to your needs.

DESIGNING YOUR OWN QUIKSHEETS

You can design your own QuikSheets according to the following rules:

- o Each sheet must have exactly 15 rows
- o Each sheet can have from one to seven columns, and each column can be either text (in which case you can enter any information that will fit into the boxes) or numeric (in which case only whole numbers can be entered into the boxes, and a total will be printed at the bottom of the column). Each column must be large enough to hold at least three characters.
- o Each sheet can have one row of check boxes, for sheets like "Things to Do."
- o You can have a maximum of 20 QuikSheets (not including the Alarm QuikSheet, which cannot be altered).

SETTING UP YOUR DISKETTES

To run QuikEditor, you'll need the following files on disk in your Macintosh:

- o A System Folder
- o The QuikEditor program
- o The QuikSheets data file

If you have enough room, copy the QuikEditor onto your main SideKick disk. If you run out of disk space, you'll probably have to set up a temporary disk with the files listed above. When the Converter program is finished, don't forget to copy the QuikSheets file back onto your SideKick disk.

STARTING QUIKEDITOR

Start the program by selecting its icon and then choosing Open from the File menu, or by double-clicking the icon.

After a moment, you should see a screen that looks something like this:

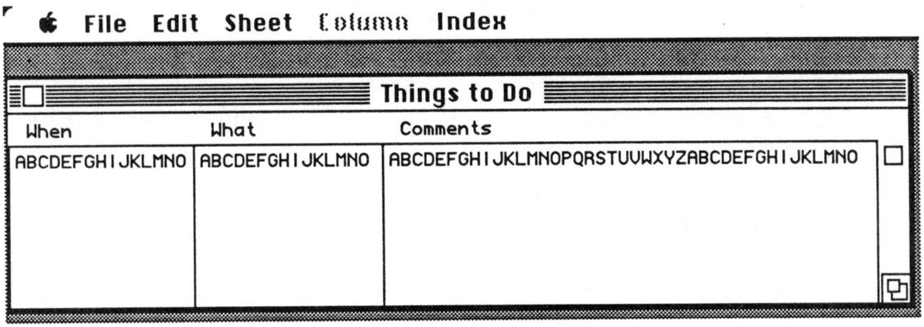

File Edit Sheet Column Index

Things to Do

When	What	Comments
ABCDEFGHIJKLMNO	ABCDEFGHIJKLMNO	ABCDEFGHIJKLMNOPQRSTUVWXYZABCDEFGHIJKLMNO

The title on the window shows you which page you are editing. The three column headings and bars show you the titles and sizes of your columns. The row of "ABCD..." letters shows you the maximum entry for each column (always an odd number of characters). This row also shows you that the columns are text. Numeric columns use "1234...". The check box to the right shows you that this sheet does have a check box. Finally, if any information was entered into your sheets, the first four rows are printed also.

You're now editing the "Things to Do" sheet. You can jump to another page by pulling down the Index menu, and select the sheet you want.

To change the total width of your QuikSheet's current columns, position the arrow over the grow box and press the mouse button. Drag the grow box to the width you want; the height won't change. When the size is correct, release the mouse button:

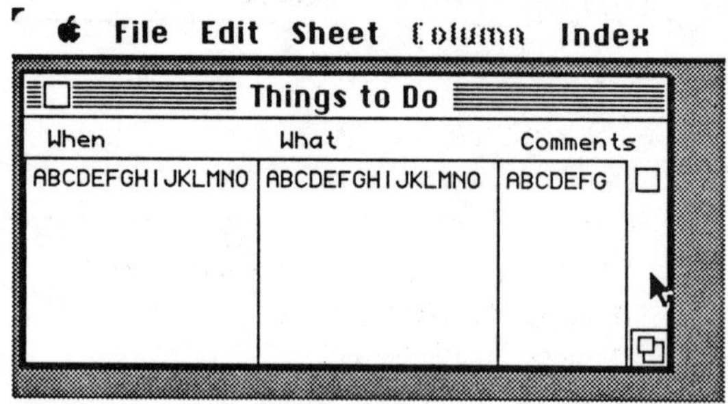

Note that QuikEditor shrunk the rightmost column to fit. If the column had been shrunk to less than three characters wide, the next column to the left would also have been shrunk.

If you want to change the way the width of the sheet is divided among the columns, position the mouse over one of the dividing lines, press the mouse button down, and drag to the new position.

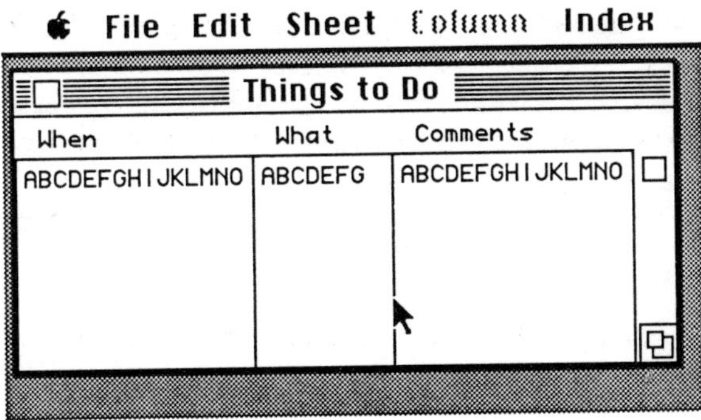

The following commands, available under the Sheet menu, act upon the entire QuikSheet.

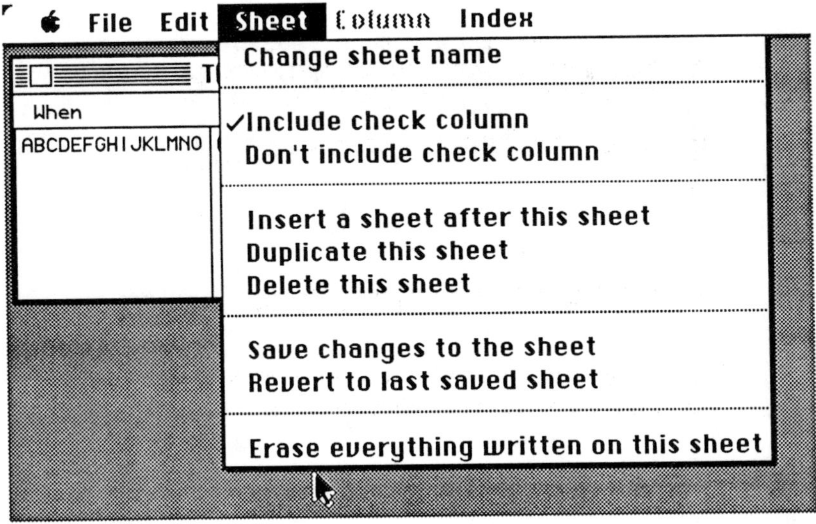

CHANGE SHEET NAME

When you make this selection, a dialog box opens up, asking you to enter a new name for the QuikSheet. Note that the new name won't actually appear in the index menu until you've saved your changes.

INCLUDE CHECK COLUMN/DON'T INCLUDE CHECK COLUMN

These two selections control whether or not the QuikSheet has a check column. Just select "Don't include..." to make the column go away.

INSERT A SHEET AFTER THIS SHEET

This will create a new QuikSheet called "Untitled," with one text column named "Untitled" after the QuikSheet you're currently editing. (There is no way to insert a QuikSheet before the "Things to Do" sheet.) It will then switch you to editing the new sheet. If you've made changes to your current sheet, you'll be given the opportunity to save them first.

DUPLICATE THIS SHEET

This creates a new QuikSheet as above, except that it has the same columns as the sheet you were working on. Any information on the QuikSheet will not be duplicated; you'll be given a blank sheet.

DELETE THIS SHEET

This will make your QuikSheet vanish. Only use this option for sheets you are sure you don't want. This command can't be reversed.

SAVE CHANGES TO THE SHEET

When you're editing a sheet, you're only modifying a copy of the sheet that your Macintosh holds in its memory; this allows you to change your mind and recover from disastrous mistakes. Therefore you must save the changed QuikSheet back into the file when you're finished. Selecting this command will save the sheet for you. (If you are about to do something that will throw away the copy in memory--such as switching to another page--you'll also be given a chance to save.)

REVERT TO LAST SAVED SHEET

This command throws out the changes since the last saved sheet--either the condition the sheet was in the last time you saved it, or the condition the sheet was in when you started if you haven't yet saved it. It is important to note that all of your changes will be permanently thrown away.

ERASE EVERYTHING WRITTEN ON THIS SHEET

This command keeps the format of the QuikSheet untouched, but will erase any information you entered into the sheet through the QuikSheet desk accessory. It's useful for such things as clearing out an expense report.

The following commands, also available under the Column menu, act on only one column. To use any of these commands, you must first click on the middle of a column (turning it black), then make your menu selection.

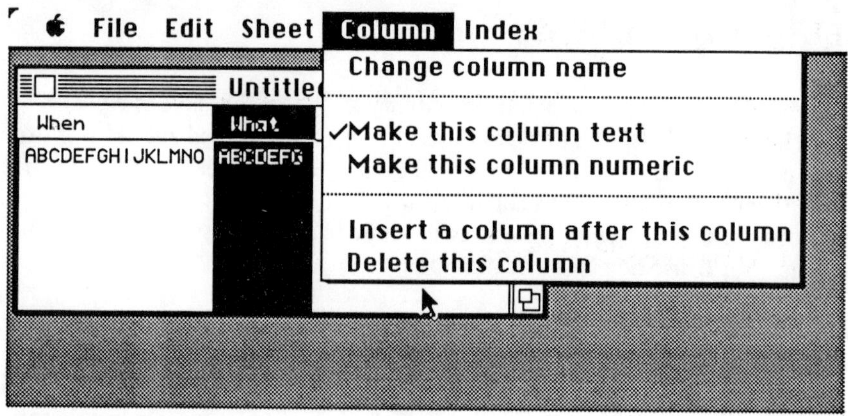

CHANGE COLUMN NAME

When you make this selection, a dialog box opens up, asking you to enter a new name for the column that has been selected.

MAKE THIS COLUMN TEXT/MAKE THIS COLUMN NUMERIC

These commands control whether the selected column is text or numeric. It only affects information that will be entered into this column in the future. If you're making a column numeric, and one of the rows already contains text information, the information will remain until you change it with the QuikSheet desk accessory.

INSERT A COLUMN AFTER THIS COLUMN

This command adds a new column after the selected column. (Again, there is no way to add a column at the start, though you could add a column in the second position, give the second column the name of the old first column, and rename the first column.) The new column will be text, have a title of "Untitled," and have a width of seven characters. It will also automatically make the QuikSheet seven characters wider.

DELETE THIS COLUMN

This command erases the currently selected column. The only way to bring this column back is to revert to the last saved sheet.

There are two other menu options of interest:

ABOUT QUIKEDITOR

This option is contained under the Apple menu, and shows you a quick reference sheet, with some of the easier-to-forget details about using QuikEditor.

CONFIGURE MACTERM

This option is contained under the File menu, and will do everything the old "Configure MacTerm" program did. It will allow you to delete the old program.

PUTTING IT ALL TOGETHER: A SIMPLE EXAMPLE

To see how everything works together, let's look at a simple example. Let's suppose you are a software developer, and need to keep track of the various pieces of equipment you use. You need to remember the name, serial number, retail cost (for insurance purposes), and ownership (you or your company) for each piece. You could start by sitting down with pen and paper, and come up with this rough sketch:

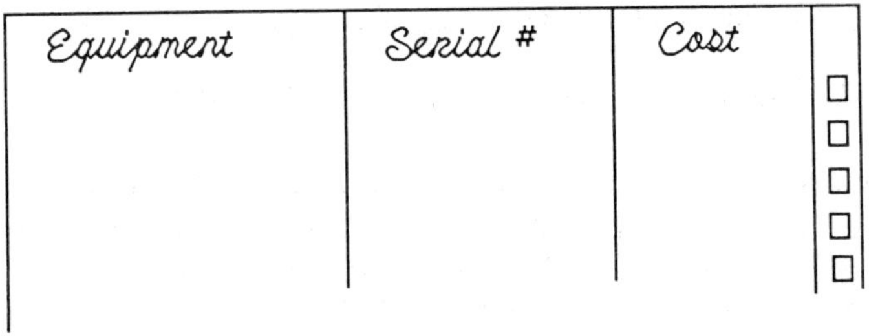

Equipment	Serial #	Cost	
			☐
			☐
			☐
			☐
			☐

You'll need fifteen characters for the equipment name, eleven characters for the serial number (you only need ten, but all widths have to be an odd number), and five characters for the cost. You'll use a row of check boxes to keep track of ownership.

Begin by starting QuikEditor. Since you want to make this the last sheet in your file, first select the last sheet listed in the Index menu ("Expenses" if you're using the file that came with your original SideKick). Then select "Insert a sheet after this sheet" from the Sheet menu. An untitled sheet will now appear:

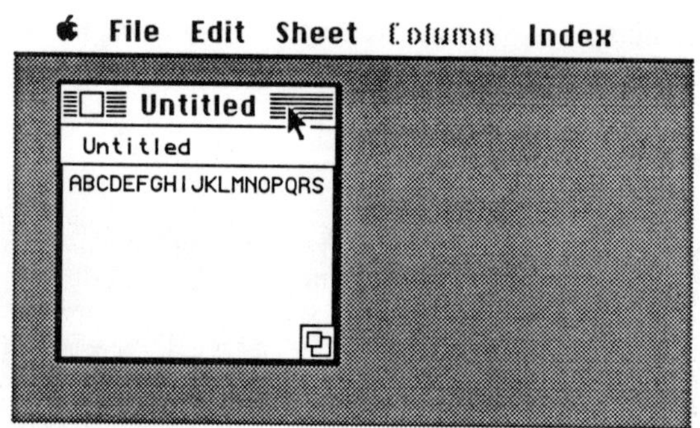

To give the sheet a proper name, select "Change sheet name" from the Sheet menu. This dialog box will now appear:

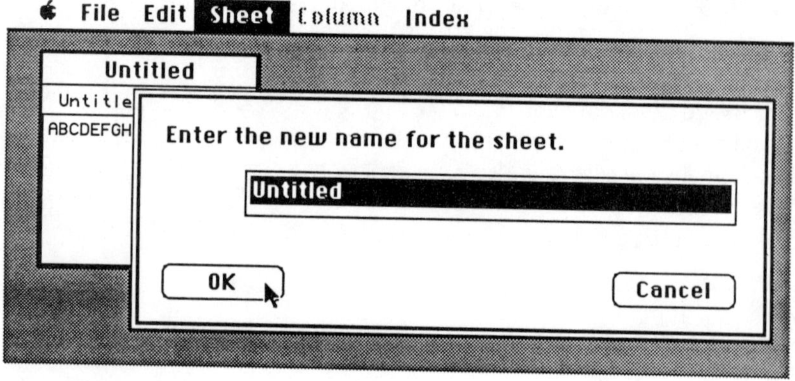

Type "My Inventory", then click in the OK button. The window will be renamed automatically to reflect your choice.

You will also want to give a name to the first column, so click in the middle of the column. The entire column should invert (white printing on a black background) and the Column menu will change from gray to black. From the Column menu, select "Change column name." Type in the name "Equipment" and click OK.

The "Equipment" column should be fifteen characters wide. A little quick counting should tell you that the column should end after the "O" in the "ABCDE..." line. Grab the grow box, and pull it in to shrink it to the appropriate size. Your screen should now look like this:

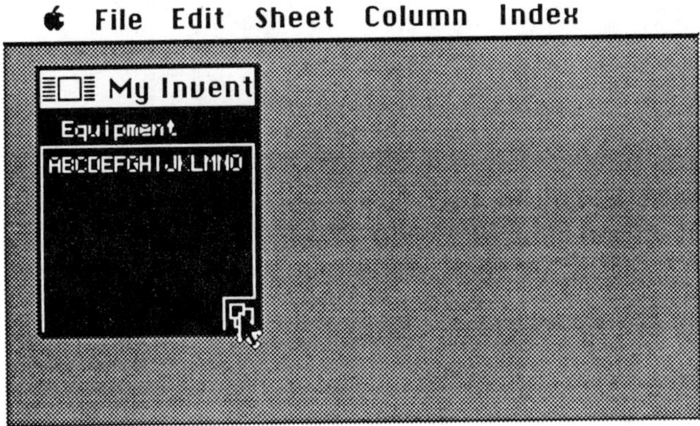

It's now time to add the serial number column. From the Column menu, select "Insert a column." Another column will now appear, seven characters wide and called "Untitled." QuikEditor automatically selects the new column, so you don't have to click on it. Select "Change column name" and type in the name ("Serial# " for this column). Grab the grow box to make the column a little wider, so that the letters are "ABCDEFGHIJK."

The third column is added in much the same way as the first. Select "Insert a column" to add the column, "Change column name" to name it "Cost," and use the grow box to shrink the column slightly to a length of five ("ABCDE"). Because this column will contain dollar amounts, select "Make this column numeric" to use numbers instead of text.

Finally, from the Sheet menu, select "Include check column" for the column of check boxes you'll use to keep track of ownership. Your screen should now look like this:

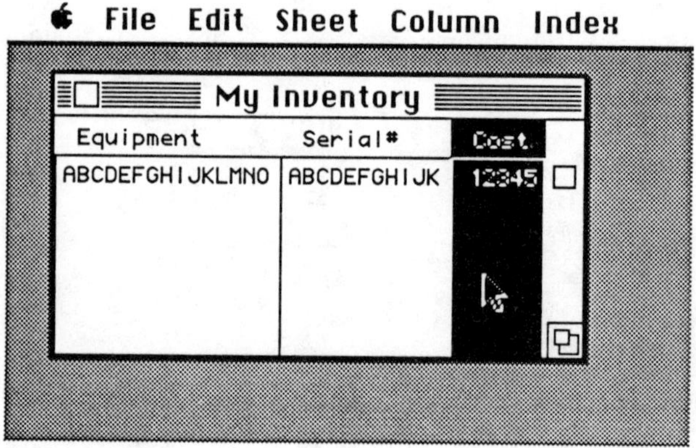

Congratulations! You've just created your first QuickSheet. All you have to do is save the sheet, and you're done!

Index

Q

R

S

T

W

Z

60 DAY MONEY-BACK GUARANTEE

CATALOG OF BORLAND PRODUCTS

4585 Scotts Valley Drive
Scotts Valley, CA 95066

Available at better dealers nationwide. Call (800) 556-2283 for the dealer nearest you. To order by Credit Card call (800) 255-8008, CA (800) 742-1133

VERSION 1.5

INFOWORLD'S SOFTWARE PRODUCT OF THE YEAR

Whether you're running WordStar™, Lotus™, dBase™, or any other program, SIDEKICK puts all these desktop accessories at your fingertips. Instantly.

A full-screen WordStar-like Editor You may jot down notes and edit files up to 25 pages long.

A Phone Directory for your names, addresses and telephone numbers. Finding a name or a number becomes a snap.

An Autodialer for all your phone calls. It will look up and dial telephone numbers for you. (A modem is required to use this function.)

A Monthly Calendar functional from year 1901 through year 2099.

A Datebook to remind you of important meetings and appointments.

A full-featured Calculator ideal for business use. It also performs decimal to hexadecimal to binary conversions.

An ASCII Table for easy reference.

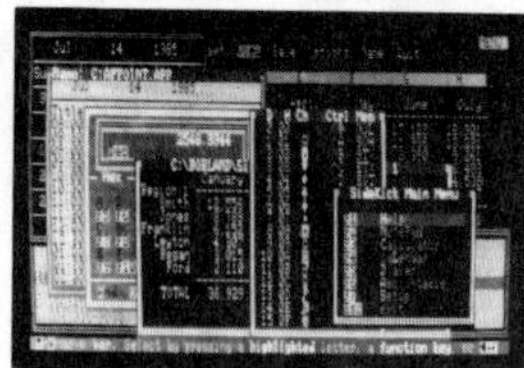

All the SIDEKICK windows stacked up over Lotus 1-2-3. From bottom to top: SIDEKICK'S "Menu Window," ASCII Table, Notepad, Calculator, Datebook, Monthly Calendar and Phone Dialer.

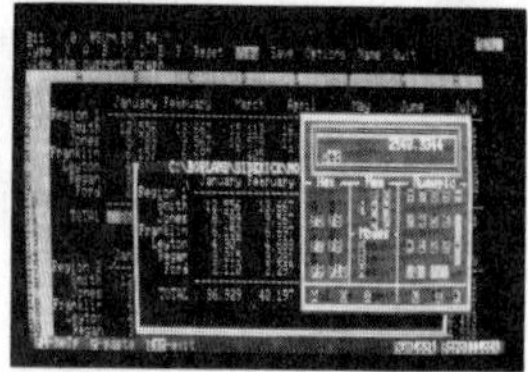

Here's SIDEKICK running over Lotus 1-2-3. In the SIDEKICK Notepad you'll notice data that's been imported directly from the Lotus screen. In the upper right you can see the Calculator.

The Critics' Choice

"In a simple, beautiful implementation of WordStar's™ block copy commands, SIDEKICK can transport all or any part of the display screen (even an area overlaid by the notepad display) to the notepad."
—Charles Petzold, PC MAGAZINE

"SIDEKICK deserves a place in every PC."
—Garry Ray, PC WEEK

"SIDEKICK is by far the best we've seen. It is also the least expensive."
—Ron Mansfield, ENTREPRENEUR

"If you use a PC, get SIDEKICK. You'll soon become dependent on it."
—Jerry Pournelle, BYTE

SIDEKICK IS AN UNPARALLELED BARGAIN AT ONLY $54.95 *(copy-protected)* OR $84.95 *(not copy-protected)*

Minimum System Configuration: SIDEKICK is available now for your IBM PC, XT, AT, PCjr., and 100% compatible microcomputers. The IBM PC jr. will only accept the SIDEKICK not copy-protected version. Your computer must have at least 128K RAM, one disk drive and PC-DOS 2.0 or greater. A Hayes™ compatible modem, IBM PCjr.™ internal modem, or AT&T® Modem 4000 is required for the autodialer function.

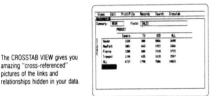

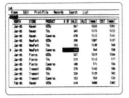

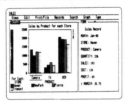

If you use an IBM PC, you need

TURBO Lightning™

Turbo Lightning™ teams up with the Random House spelling Dictionary® to check your spelling as you type!

Turbo Lightning, using the 83,000-word Random House Dictionary, checks your spelling *as you type*. If you misspell a word, it alerts you with a 'beep'. At the touch of a key, *Turbo* Lightning opens a window on top of your application program and suggests the correct spelling. Just press ENTER and the misspelled word is instantly replaced with the correct word. It's that easy!

Turbo Lightning works hand-in-hand with the Random House Thesaurus® to give you instant access to synonyms.

Turbo Lightning lets you choose just the right word from a list of alternates, so you don't say the same thing the same way every time. Once *Turbo* Lightning opens the Thesaurus window, you see a list of alternate words, organized by parts of speech. You just select the word you want, press ENTER and your new word will instantly replace the original word. Pure magic!

If you ever write a word, think a word, or say a word, you need Turbo Lightning.

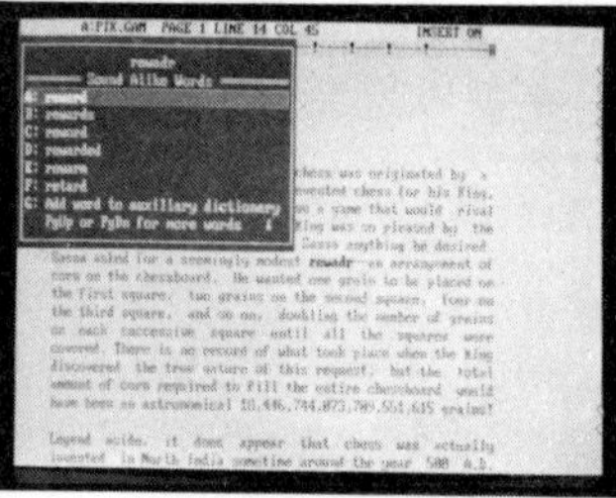

The Turbo Lightning Dictionary.

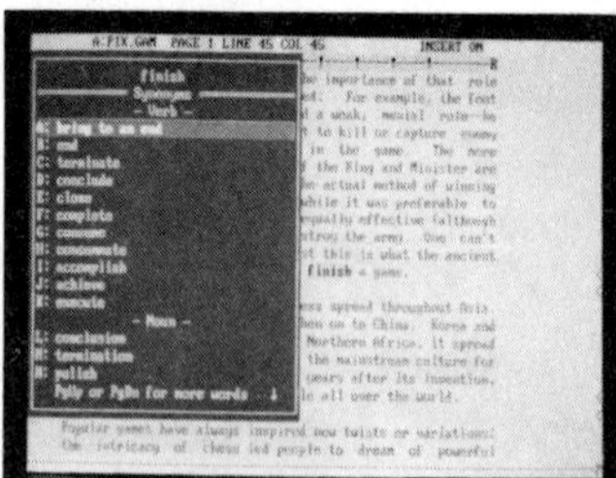

The Turbo Lightning Thesaurus.

Turbo Lightning's intelligence lets you teach it new words. The more you use Turbo Lightning, the smarter it gets!

You can also *teach* your new *Turbo* Lightning your name, business associates' names, street names, addresses, correct capitalizations, and any specialized words you use frequently. Teach *Turbo Lightning* once, and it knows forever.

Turbo Lightning™ is the engine that powers Borland's Turbo Lightning Library™.

Turbo Lightning brings electronic power to the Random House Dictionary® and Random House Thesaurus®. They're at your fingertips —even while you're running other programs. *Turbo* Lightning will also 'drive' soon-to-be-released encyclopedias, extended thesauruses, specialized dictionaries, and many other popular reference works. You get a head start with this first volume in the *Turbo* Lightning Library.

And because *Turbo* Lightning is a Borland product, you know you can rely on our quality, our 60-day money-back guarantee, and our eminently fair prices.

BORLAND
INTERNATIONAL

Suggested Retail Price $99.95
(not copy-protected)

Minimum System Requirements:
128K IBM PC® or 100% compatible computer, with 2 floppy disk drives and PC-DOS (MS-DOS) 2.0 or greater.

TURBO *GRAPHIX* TOOLBOX™

HIGH RESOLUTION GRAPHICS AND GRAPHIC WINDOW MANAGEMENT

FOR THE IBM PC

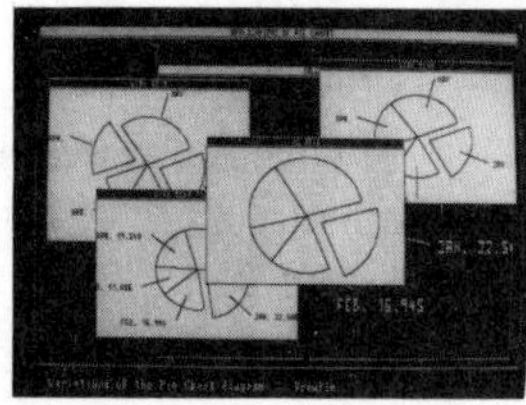

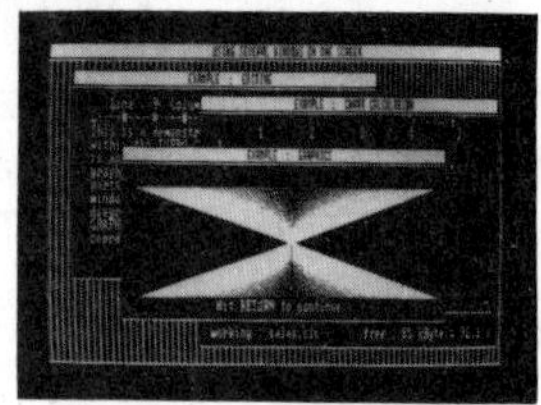

Dazzling graphics and painless windows.

The Turbo Graphix Toolbox™ will give even a beginning programmer the expert's edge. It's a complete library of Pascal procedures that include:

- Full graphics window management.
- Tools that allow you to draw and hatch pie charts, bar charts, circles, rectangles and a full range of geometric shapes.
- Procedures that save and restore graphic images to and from disk.
- Functions that allow you to precisely plot curves.
- Tools that allow you to create animation or solve those difficult curve fitting problems.

No sweat and no royalties.

You can incorporate part, or all of these tools in your programs, and yet, we won't charge you any royalties. Best of all, these functions and procedures come complete with source code on disk ready to compile!

John Markoff & Paul Freiberger, syndicated columnists:

"While most people only talk about low-cost personal computer software, Borland has been doing something about it. And Borland provides good technical support as part of the price."

Turbo Graphix Toolbox—only $54.95 *(not copy protected).*

Minimum System Configuration: Turbo Graphix Toolbox is available today for your computer running Turbo Pascal 2.0 or greater for PC-DOS, or truly compatible MS-DOS. Your computer must have at least 128K RAM, one disk drive and PC-DOS 2.0 or greater, and MS-DOS 2.0 or greater with IBM Graphics Adapter or Enhanced Graphics Adapter, IBM-compatible Graphics Adapter, or Hercules Graphics Card.

TURBO EDITOR TOOLBOX

It's All You Need To Build Your Own Text Editor Or Word Processor.

Build your own lightning-fast editor and incorporate it into your Turbo Pascal programs. Turbo Editor Toolbox™ gives you easy-to-install modules. Now you can integrate a fast and powerful editor into your own programs. You get the source code, the manual and the know how.

Create your own word processor. We provide all the editing routines. You plug in the features you want. You could build a WordStar®-like editor with pull-down menus like Microsoft's® Word, and make it work as fast as WordPerfect™.

To demonstrate the tremendous power of Turbo Editor Toolbox, we give you the source code for two sample editors:

Simple Editor A complete editor ready to include in your programs. With windows, block commands, and memory-mapped screen routines.

MicroStar™ A full-blown text editor with a complete pull-down menu user interface, plus a lot more. Modify MicroStar's pull-down menu system and include it in your Turbo Pascal programs.

The Turbo Editor Toolbox gives you all the standard features you would expect to find in any word processor:

- Word wrap
- UNDO last change
- Auto indent
- Find and Find/Replace with options
- Set left and right margin
- Block mark, move and copy.
- Tab, insert and overstrike modes, centering, etc.

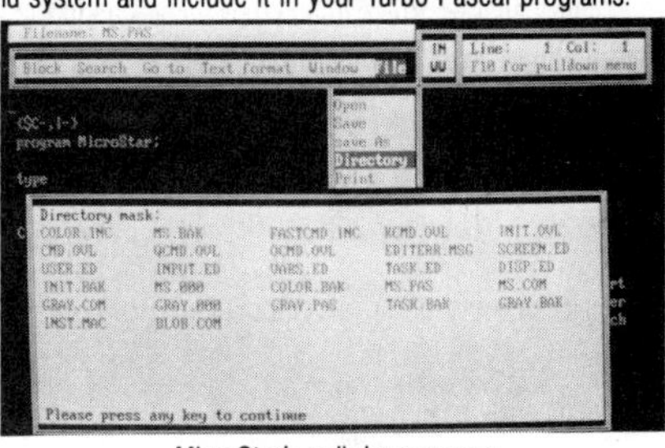

MicroStar's pull-down menus.

And Turbo Editor Toolbox has features that word processors selling for several hundred dollars can't begin to match. Just to name a few:

- ☑ ***RAM-based editor***. You can edit very large files and yet editing is lightning fast.
- ☑ ***Memory-mapped screen routines.*** Instant paging, scrolling and text display.
- ☑ ***Keyboard installation.*** Change control keys from WordStar-like commands to any that you prefer.
- ☑ ***Multiple windows.*** See and edit up to eight documents—or up to eight parts of the same document—all at the same time.
- ☑ ***Multi-Tasking.*** Automatically save your text. Plug in a digital clock . . . an appointment alarm—see how it's done with MicroStar's "background" printing.

Best of all, **source code is included for everything in the Editor Toolbox.** Use any of the Turbo Editor Toolbox's features in your programs. And pay no royalties.

Minimum system configuration: The Turbo Editor Toolbox requires an IBM PC, XT, AT, 3270, PCjr or true compatible with a minimum 192K RAM, running PC-DOS (MS-DOS) 2.0 or greater. You must be using Turbo Pascal 3.0 for IBM and compatibles.

Suggested Retail Price $69.95 (not copy-protected)